U.S. Strategic Trade

U.S. Strategic Trade

An Export Control System for the 1990s

Senator John Heinz

Westview Press

BOULDER • SAN FRANCISCO • OXFORD

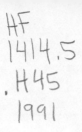

Tables 4.2 and 4.3, p.110, are used with permission of the copyright holder, Morgan Guaranty Trust Company of New York.

This Westview softcover edition is printed on acid-free paper and bound in library-quality, coated covers that carry the highest rating of the National Association of State Textbook Administrators, in consultation with the Association of American Publishers and the Book Manufacturers' Institute.

Published in 1991 in the United States of America by Westview Press, Inc., 5500 Central Avenue, Boulder, Colorado 80301, and in the United Kingdom by Westview Press, 36 Lonsdale Road, Summertown, Oxford OX2 7EW

Library of Congress Cataloging-in-Publication Data
Heinz, John, 1938-
    U.S. strategic trade : an export control system for the 1990s /
John Heinz.
        p. cm.
    Includes bibliographical references and index.
    ISBN 0-8133-8126-6
    1. Export controls--United States. 2. United States--Commercial
policy. 3. National security--United States. 4. Foreign trade
regulation--United States. I. Title.
HF1414.5.H45   1991
382'.64'0973--dc20   90-21889
                                                                     CIP

Printed and bound in the United States of America

The paper used in this publication meets the requirements of the American National Standard for Permanence of Paper for Printed Library Materials Z39.48-1984.

10   9   8   7   6   5   4   3   2   1

Contents

Foreword

Senator John Heinz (R-PA) has long been recognized as one of the most knowledgeable members of Congress on the subject of the U.S. export control system. In this timely book the senator once again demonstrates his scholarship and encyclopedic comprehension of this subject as he presents a thorough review of U.S. and allied export control policies since World War II. The study presents a clear, historical perspective of how we got into the bureaucratic logjam we are in today, but it also lays out a blueprint for how we might reorganize the government in order to extricate ourselves.

In 1979, in 1985, and again in 1989, Senator Heinz played a leading role in legislating reforms of the export administration system. As the chief staff member of his Banking Subcommittee on International Finance and Monetary Policy and later as the assistant secretary for trade policy and as the under secretary for export administration in the Commerce Department, I can also attest to the impact of the reform amendments Senator Heinz authored. For example, as a result of the tougher criteria and findings he was able to legislate in the area of foreign policy controls, the administration decided not to use such sanctions as a first option in response to a number of foreign policy crisis situations. Instead, policymakers utilized other means of expressing U.S. government disapproval of other countries' behavior or policies, thus avoiding actions that might further damage the reputation of the United States as a reliable supplier of goods and services. I can attest to the fact that the foreign availability function began to play a more effective role in decontrolling goods kept far beyond their useful lives as strategic items because of reforms set in motion by Senator Heinz in the 1985 amendments to the Export Administration Act.

Obviously, however, much remains to be done. Although foreign availability succeeded in finally decontrolling items such as the 80286-based microcomputer, the system remains gridlocked on other foreign availability decisions and in many other areas, such as commodity jurisdiction disputes between the Commerce Department and the

Departments of State and Defense.

Unlike many books about Washington that provide critiques of what is wrong but offer no solutions to set things right, this study provides a practical plan for the reorganization of the export control function now spread among the Departments of Commerce, Defense, and State. Senator Heinz presents a compelling argument for elevating export administration to a new, higher role as a key element in U.S. defense and foreign policy and then goes on to argue that such an elevation and consolidation would provide the prompt and decisive answers to licensing requests that U.S. exporters need and deserve. With export licensing accounting for more than $100 billion in U.S. trade in 1989 and with it likely to continue to be needed for tens of billions of dollars in trade for the immediate future, our nation can afford no lesser system.

If it is true that the Cold War is over and that the United States has won it, as President Ronald Reagan is reported to have said on his trip back from the Reykjavik, Iceland, summit meeting, then it is appropriate to give at least partial credit for that victory to the part played by the Coordinating Committee for Multilateral Export Controls and the export control system that has been in place since 1949. The question remains, however, whether the cost of that victory is higher than it might have been under an alternative strategy and whether that cost, in terms of delay and confusion, must be continued into the future. Senator Heinz addresses this question, considering how we can best organize ourselves to reap the fruits of that victory and to maintain the peace through technological security. The challenge is to accomplish all this while at the same time ensuring our nation's economic competitiveness.

To govern is to choose, and no decision is more important to our survival and our success as a nation than the balance that must be struck between national security and economic prosperity. In this book Senator Heinz provides a practical and understandable blueprint for helping our nation's decisionmakers achieve that compromise.

Paul Freedenberg

Preface

I like the dreams of the future better than the history of the past.
                                                              --Thomas Jefferson

The genesis of this book dates back to June 1989, when I was invited by the Center for Strategic and International Studies to speak before a forum on East-West economics. I was asked to address two themes: the pressures from allies and industry to narrow export controls to the Soviet bloc, and the impact of Soviet President and Party Secretary-General Mikhail Gorbachev's reform movement on U.S. export control policy toward the Soviet bloc.

The invitation fortuitously dovetailed with a decision Senator Jake Garn (R-UT) and I had reached earlier in the year to introduce a bill to reform the U.S. export control system. Since 1977 I have had a role in nurturing the growth of the current U.S. national security export control system, at various times as chairman or ranking member of the Subcommittee on International Finance and Monetary Policy of the Senate Banking Committee that oversees export controls. I particularly remember the contentious times surrounding the reauthorization of the Export Administration Act of 1979 and its subsequent reauthorizations in 1983 and 1985 and the 1988 Trade Bill.

When it comes to the U.S. national security export control system, I cannot help but identify with Thomas Jefferson's remark. I will be among the first to admit that the system, with its long history of tortuous growth and anachronistic policies and appendages, must be reformed if the United States is to avoid the problems of the past. For this reason, Senator Garn and I introduced a bill, the Export Administration Act of 1990, which had as its centerpiece the creation of the Office of Strategic Trade and Technology (OSTT--hereafter, the OSTT Bill). The OSTT Bill would create a new national security export control system to make sweeping changes in the process by which our nation arrives at decisions on export controls and technology matters. The organizational structure and policy changes in the OSTT Bill are discussed in Chapter 6 of this book.

This country can no longer afford the *status quo*. Export control policy is central to our national defense and defense industrial base, to our balance of trade and the health of our high technology sector, and to the success of our foreign policy with respect to our closest allies in NATO, developing nations, and the Warsaw Pact. With a sea change occurring in Eastern Europe and the Soviet Union and major uncertainty about the future course of events in China, the opportunity to lead--and the responsibility of leadership--has never been greater. The choices we make will not merely affect our relations with the East for a generation; our choices can revitalize our relations with our allies, strengthen our common sense of purpose, and restore our eroding position of leadership.

John Heinz

Acknowledgments

I especially wish to acknowledge the contributions of my staff members, Bill Reinsch, Dennis Culkin, and Andres D. Onate, with whom I have worked over the years on the subject of this book. Their review and critique of portions of this work were invaluable. I am deeply grateful to Allison Cessna for so expertly assembling the final manuscript. The views expressed in this book are my own.

J. H.

About the Author

John Heinz (R-PA) is Pennsylvania's senior senator. He was first elected to the U.S. Senate in 1976 and was reelected in 1982 and 1988. Between 1971 and 1976, he served Pennsylvania's 18th Congressional District in the House of Representatives. Senator Heinz has long argued that the United States needs to do a better job of defending vital economic interests against the unfair trading practices of other nations. He introduced eight bills that became part of the 1988 Omnibus Trade and Competitiveness Bill, which plays an important role in this book. He also authored the Export Trading Company Act of 1982, the Export Administration Amendments Act of 1985, and the export financing "war chest" program established in 1986.

During the first session of the 101st Congress, Senator Heinz sponsored or cosponsored legislation dealing with the controversial U.S.-Japan Fighter Support Experimental Program, the U.S.-Korean Fighter Program, the Missile Technology Control and Equipment Act of 1989 (S. 1924), the Chemical and Biological Weapons Control Act of 1989 (S. 8), an amendment to S. 8 to strengthen the Australia Group's role in controlling chemical agents and precursors, the Defense Production Act of 1990, the Biological Weapons Control Act, an amendment calling for a report on confidence-building measures regarding technology transfer and direct investments in Poland and Hungary, and, finally, along with Senator Jake Garn (R-UT), the Export Administration Act of 1990, which established the Office of Strategic Trade and Technology.

Introduction

It is time to move beyond containment.

--President George Bush, May 12, 1989

The Problem: Peace as the New Challenge to
U.S. Export Control Policy

Peace, it has become commonplace to say, is breaking out all over--in Central and Eastern Europe, Afghanistan, Ethiopia, Cambodia, and Angola. The benefits to be reaped are enticing, both for fiscal reasons and global peace. A *Washington Post* editorial put it this way: "The last time peace broke out was after the Vietnam War. Then as now, there was much excited talk of a peace dividend from declining defense expenditures. . . . To the extent that [President Bush] seriously cuts the defense budget, he creates, if not a peace dividend, nonetheless a different world."[1]

The question that confronts the U.S. government and Congress today is whether the U.S. export control system is up to the task of meeting the challenges it will surely face in the 1990s. The evolution of the current system is not very encouraging.

The U.S. export control system had its origins in trade "security controls" imposed during World Wars I and II and fine-tuned during the Cold War. Throughout the past forty years, the U.S. industrial-military-nuclear export control system has been challenged, with various degrees of success and failure, by such issues as the military threat to the security of the United States and its allies; the threat of shortages of key industrial resources; "economic defense" (a 1950s euphemism for economic warfare and embargoes); foreign policy concerns over nonproliferation of nuclear, missile, and chemical weapons; and, more recently, the economic security of the United States (the health of the U.S. industrial base).

One thing is clear: U.S. export control policy has never faced the challenge of addressing national and economic security interests in a period of nuclear and conventional arms reductions, declining defense budgets, the potential transformation of rival defense alliances, the inexorable global movement toward democracy, the integration of world markets, rampant U.S. and Third World debt, and the global high technology boom. Indeed, this is all occurring at a time when the very bases of the Cold War are in question. On May 12, 1989, at Texas A&M University, President George Bush announced in his first Soviet policy address that, "now it is time to move beyond containment, to a new policy for the 1990s--one that recognizes the full scope of change taking place around the world and in the Soviet Union itself. . . . In sum, the United States now has as its goal much more than simply containing Soviet expansionism--we seek the integration of the Soviet Union into the community of nations."[2] Just as President Harry Truman proclaimed the start of the Cold War in 1947, so President Bush took the first step to proclaim its end in 1989.

In addition, the emergence of Mikhail Gorbachev's "new thinking" (i.e., *perestroika* and *glasnost*) has greatly reduced--if not eliminated--the role of Marxist-Leninist ideological thinking as a determinant of international relations. Gone, it seems, are the primacy of the so-called universal truths of Marxism-Leninism: the class struggle and the dictatorship of the proletariat, historical and dialectical materialism, and imperialism.

In this book I maintain that "a different world" will require a different approach to export controls. But moving beyond the rhetoric, as we shall see, may be more difficult. The vision of a different world will also require a vision of the various instruments needed to achieve it.

Trends and an Agenda for the 1990s

As the 1990s begin, the broadening of the national security basis of the U.S. export control system beyond military matters converges with well-defined geopolitical and technological trends to increase pressure on the United States to narrow or eliminate export controls West-East and West-West. These trends, combined with several contentious control issues, make up a formidable agenda. Consider the following:

1. decreasing geopolitical tensions in Europe and a corresponding increase in pressure on the United States from COCOM members to remove or relax significantly current strategic trade restrictions to the Soviet bloc, particularly Poland and Hungary;
2. up to the time of the Tiananmen massacre, a decreasing, if not vanishing, view of China as a threat to the national security of the

United States and the Western alliance and a corresponding increase in pressure on the United States to remove China from the COCOM-proscribed list or to establish a shorter control list (Despite secret missions and other early U.S. efforts to move beyond Tiananmen, it remains to be seen just how much ground China lost in COCOM.);

3. increasing pressure on the United States, mainly from domestic sources, to narrow or eliminate its export controls West-West, which account for over 80 percent of U.S. trade, coupled with the corresponding decrease in confidence in the U.S. government toward the current export enforcement systems of COCOM member states;

4. increasing pressures to expand the scope of Western export control regimes (the "foreign-policy-control-of-the-day" syndrome) to take into account Third World pursuit of missile and chemical weapons technologies and the potential decline in cooperation by Western suppliers in preventing missile and chemical weapons proliferation; and

5. increasing globalization, commoditization, and foreign availability of technologies outside the Western alliance, a trend noted by the National Research Council, and decreasing markets, declining exports, and loss of technology leadership by U.S. industry.[3]

The Focus

Export controls are an integral part of U.S. foreign economic policy. Like tariffs, credits, quotas, boycotts, embargoes, loans, and currency manipulation, export controls are economic instruments of foreign policy that may be used for purposes of persuasion, reward, or punishment in order to influence the internal politics or foreign actions of another state. Export controls as economic instruments of policy were conceived, as we shall see, generally for the purpose of depriving real or potential enemies of scarce resources and denying them access to U.S. and Western high technology that significantly improves their military potential.

Export controls are also political and economic lightning rods. These are times of skyrocketing foreign trade and domestic budget deficits, declining exports, declining defense budgets in the United States and the Soviet Union, the technology explosion abroad, and protective import policies by many U.S. trading partners. U.S. export control policy is seen both at home and abroad as unnecessarily restrictive. As a consequence, the United States has attracted more than its share of problems regarding the economic impact of export controls. During Secretary of State James Baker III's initial visit to Europe to discuss NATO-related issues, he heard more European complaints about the restrictiveness of U.S. export control policy than other comparable senior officials in recent memory.[4]

Domestically, the 1987 National Academy of Science study of the U.S. national security export control system fueled the fire considerably with its finding that U.S. export controls cost the country $9.3 billion in lost profits on export and foreign sales, and 188,000 jobs.[5] The President's Commission on Industrial Competitiveness estimated that foreign policy controls alone cost $4.7 billion annually in lost sales.[6]

Export controls cost money. This, if anything, is why this area of our national security deserves as much scrutiny as NATO's future role in Europe. Currently, the three frontline agencies (Commerce, Defense, and State) total nearly 1,000 personnel with a combined budget of almost $50 million to process 150,000 export license applications annually. Only about 1 percent of these require special attention: The value of the nearly 1,500 licenses is about $1.5 billion, nothing to sneer at, but hardly the stuff that justifies the magnitude of the system in place today.

Finally, export controls are an excellent bellwether to geopolitical relations. Since 1949, U.S. export control findings and policies have been piled one on top of the other, much like archeological strata. Each stratum says something about the politics and economics of the times. By peeling off each one and looking at it from the perspective of the Congressional findings that determined U.S. export control policy for that particular time frame, this book hopes to shed some light on the incremental development of export control policies that may or may not be relevant in the 1990s.

All of the above factors are contributing to the increasing unmanageability of the U.S. export control system. The incremental growth of Congressional findings to support the proliferation of export control policies in the past forty years, the interlocking and sometimes adversarial relationship between the United States and COCOM (which, in my view, is reaching a crossroads), and global geopolitical and economic changes, all pose a formidable agenda for the next decade. It is my thesis that the extent to which U.S. export control and technology transfer policies and procedures succeed in the next decade will depend on the ability of the leadership of the United States to keep pace with changes that are rocking the world today.

But let me be clear: Nothing in the developments today argue for the dismantling of the U.S. or COCOM export control systems. I certainly do not make this argument. On the contrary, I find it necessary to continue export controls toward the Soviet Union, the Warsaw Pact, and, to a large extent, China. But I do argue that there are numerous unnecessary controls both on the controlled countries and on friendly countries. Many of these policies are illogical, outdated, and unfair and create unfortunate adversarial relationships between government and industry and between friendly governments. There is also a lack of foresight regarding the relationship between U.S. national and economic security interests. Most importantly, U.S. export control policy is still wedded to the narrow and traditional notion of national security--the Soviet Union. It is time to broaden this notion to include hostage-taking, terrorism, drug trafficking, and even environmental issues.

Scope and Organization

Chapter 1 traces the evolution of U.S. export control policies and procedures since 1949, focusing in the main on the three Export Administration Acts since 1949. The legal basis for the U.S. export control system is discussed, as well as the offices with oversight for munitions, dual-use, and nuclear energy controls. The first chapter also looks at the length and complexities of the U.S. control lists, commodity jurisdiction disputes, the licensing maze, organizational growth pains, and critiques of the U.S. export control system from private and government studies as well as the export industry itself. My own views of the system conclude this chapter.

Chapter 2 discusses the origins of COCOM, its functions, and the politics of multilateral export controls and looks at another little-known export control system, the Battle Act, which provided the legal basis for U.S. cooperation in COCOM.

Chapter 3 examines the basis for maintaining or liberalizing the U.S. national security export control system by analyzing the U.S. and COCOM's export control policies toward the Soviet Union, the Warsaw Pact, and China.

Chapter 4 looks at "economic security"--a new basis for the U.S. national security export control system. This chapter explores the discrete issues that make up the concept of "economic security," including the U.S. defense and technology base, the Defense Production Act, foreign direct investments, the acquisition of defense-related firms, the Committee on Foreign Investments in the United States (CFIUS), declining exports, trade barriers, and foreign availability.

Chapter 5 examines several key technology transfer and export control issues whose resolution or lack thereof holds the key to the viability of the U.S. control system and COCOM in the decade ahead. This chapter considers the future of COCOM, the related problems of streamlining and enforcement policies, foreign availability, emerging technologies, and the expansion of the traditional notion of national security by looking at the impact of missile and chemical weapons proliferation on U.S. foreign policy.

Chapter 6 discusses the Office of Strategic Trade and Technology in the context of the findings and recommendations made in Chapters 2 through 5.

This book and the OSTT Bill are intended to spur a much-needed debate on U.S. export control policy in the 1990s as Congress holds hearings on the reauthorization of the Export Administration Act of 1979, which expired on September 30, 1990.

Notes

1. Editorial, *Washington Post*, November 29, 1989.

2. President George Bush, "Change in the Soviet Union," an address by the President at the Texas A&M University commencement ceremony, College Station, Texas, May 12, 1989, Current Policy No. 1175 (Washington, D.C.: U.S. Department of State, Bureau of Public Affairs, May 1989).

3. National Research Council, *Global Trends in Computer Technology and Their Impact on Export Control* (Washington, D.C.: National Academy Press, 1988).

4. *Defense News*, February 20, 1989, p. 8.

5. National Academy of Sciences (NAS), *Balancing the National Interest: U.S. National Security Export Controls and Global Economic Competition* (Washington, D.C.: National Academy Press, 1987). See Appendix D, pp. 254-277, for an explanation of the methodology used to arrive at these figures. In all fairness, the NAS concedes that the methodology had its shortcomings and that the results should be read with several qualifications in mind. Because of the controversy surrounding the economic impact of export controls, the NAS opted to omit a similar attempt to estimate the economic impact of export controls in a second study commissioned by Congress under the 1988 Omnibus Trade Bill.

6. The figures are from the President's report entitled *Global Competition: The New Reality*, as cited in U.S. Department of Commerce, *Report of the President's Export Council Subcommittee on Export Administration, 1985-1989*, Vol. 2 (Washington, D.C.: U.S. Government Printing Office, 1989), p. 35.

#100   04-01-2017 4:57PM
Item(s) checked out to p28492092.

TITLE: U.S. strategic trade : an export
CALL #: HF1414.5 .H45 1991
BARCODE: 3 0800 02405 9294
DUE DATE: 10-14-17

King Library Hours
    th 8-9, Fri-Sat 9-6, Sun 1-7

1

The Origins and Evolution of the U.S. Export Control System

Origins

The origins of the U.S. export control system lie in the period spanning World War I and World War II. Wartime export controls regulated primarily munitions equipment and services. Following is a sketch of the three most important legislative antecedents to the comprehensive export control system enacted in 1949.

Trading with the Enemy Act, 1917

The TWEA authorized the President to restrict the export of munitions items to the enemy. In 1933 the TWEA was amended to apply both to wartime and national emergency conditions. In December 1950, President Truman invoked the TWEA to impose a freeze on Chinese and North Korean assets and to institute an embargo against the two countries after the outbreak of war on the Korean peninsula. China was removed from the jurisdiction of the TWEA in 1980.

The TWEA is administered by the Office of Foreign Assets Control (OFAC) of the Department of the Treasury. Today, the only countries remaining under its jurisdiction are Cambodia, Vietnam, Cuba, North Korea, Estonia, Latvia, and Lithuania. Funds of Estonia, Latvia, and Lithuania were frozen during the war period and remain so because the United States does not recognize the incorporation of the Baltic states into the Soviet Union. The TWEA provides for ten years imprisonment and a $50,000 fine for violations.

Treasury also administers the International Emergency Economic Powers Act (IEEPA), which grants the President virtually the same authority during peacetime that TWEA confers during wartime. IEEPA is or has been applied in embargoes against Iran, Nicaragua, South Africa, Libya, and Panama.

To avoid duplicative licensing responsibilities, Treasury and Commerce generally reach agreement on which authority will issue licenses. In cases where Treasury issues licenses, Commerce recognizes them as having been granted under the EAA. IEEPA provides for ten years imprisonment and a $50,000 fine for violations.[1]

Neutrality Act of 1935

In 1935 President Franklin Roosevelt signed the Neutrality Act, which provided the first legal basis for the export of munitions products and services.[2] The purpose of the export control provisions of the act was to regulate the fast-growing, multibillion-dollar *commercial* arms export industry. From the adoption of the act to the outbreak of World War II, the munitions control office issued licenses valued at approximately $1.2 billion.

The act provided for a munitions licensing system and a munitions control list (the International Traffic in Arms Regulations, ITAR). The secretary of state administered the ITAR through the Office of Arms and Munitions Control, the forerunner to today's Office of Munitions Control (OMC).[3] Licenses could only be denied if the proposed export violated U.S. law; national security considerations were not yet the primary reasons for denying exports, although the secretary was empowered to invoke this as a condition for denial.

The 1935 act was replaced no less than seven times, culminating in the International Security Assistance and Arms Export Control Act of 1976, the current legal basis for regulating commercial arms exports.

Export Control Act of 1940

According to the State Department, "the history of general United States export controls may be said to have begun" on July 2, 1940, when shortly after the fall of France (June 22, 1940), the Congress gave the President blanket authority to impose export controls on twenty-nine materials under the Act to Expedite the Strengthening of the National Defense.[4] The 1940 act instituted a licensing regime to restrict the export of military equipment or munitions items as well as component parts, machine tools, or materials necessary for their manufacture, servicing, or operation. The act was extended annually until February 28, 1949, when the Export Control Act was enacted.

Between 1945 and 1947, two decontrol acts and the "general anticipation of excess capacity in most industries brought about a rapid relaxation of export restrictions."[5] Controls were maintained on materials in short supply (steel, chemicals, drugs, and building supplies), munitions, and nuclear energy materials.[6]

The year 1947 emerged as the watershed for extending the export control system to cover national security concerns. Scarce resources, the fall of Czechoslovakia in March 1947, and the announcement of the Marshall Plan in June 1947 served as the immediate catalysts for the U.S. government's decision to renew and strengthen the 1940 act. These same Congressional findings, as we shall see, also led to a policy to seek international cooperation to institute a multilateral export control system to protect the transfer of scarce materials and equipment from the United States to Europe (discussed in Chapter 2).[7]

Evolution of the Export Control System, 1949-1989

Since 1949 the U.S. export control system has evolved incrementally along three tracks: dual-use, munitions, and nuclear export controls. Table 1.1 lists the three and their legal bases.

Dual-Use Export Controls: The Controversial Track

Export controls on munitions items and nuclear energy equipment and technologies have historically enjoyed a higher consensual base at home and abroad because the controlled items are highly identifiable and therefore less controversial. Criticisms of munitions and nuclear export controls generally focus on the administration of the controls rather than on the exportability or nonexportability of the products in question, be they missiles or nuclear reactors.

Unfortunately, the same cannot be said for dual-use technologies and commodities, which may have both commercial and military application. It is not uncommon for some items to appear on two or more of the control lists. For example, computers in their various manifestations may be controlled by all three lists, aircraft engines by two of the lists. Commodity jurisdiction disputes have become commonplace in the 1980s and promise to become even more prevalent in the 1990s as commercially emerging new technologies also possess military applications.

TABLE 1.1
Legal Bases of the U.S. Export Control System

	State Department	Commerce Department	Energy Department
Oversight office	Office of Munitions Control	Bureau of Export Administration	Nuclear Regulatory Commission
Legal authority	International Traffic In Arms Regulations; Arms Export Control Act	Export Administration Regulations; Export Administration Act	Atomic Energy Act; Nuclear Non-Proliferation Act
Control lists	U.S. Munitions List	Commodity Control List	Nuclear Referral List (with Commerce)

The section that follows examines the three acts that account for the present dual-use control system: the Export Control Act of 1949, the Export Administration Act of 1969, and the Export Administration Act of 1979, as amended, which is still in force.

Export Control Act of 1949

The Export Control Act of 1949 can only be understood against the background of the Cold War. In the immediate postwar period, the U.S. government turned its attention to reviving the traditional pattern of prewar East-West trade to aid in the recovery of Europe. The United States looked toward Eastern Europe for raw materials in short supply such as fuel, foodstuffs, and timber. In return, the United States was prepared to export machinery, equipment, and consumer goods that were in short supply in Eastern Europe.[8]

Prewar East-West trade was relatively small. In 1938, for example, trade between the countries that became known as the "Soviet bloc" and the free world totaled approximately $3.3 billion, or 7.4 percent of world trade. Western European countries' trade with Eastern Europe was about 8.1 percent of the former's total trade. In 1938 the countries of Western Europe imported slightly more than $1 billion worth of goods from the European Soviet bloc countries and exported $775 million in return. Capital goods constituted more than 50 percent of the total shipments from Western to Eastern Europe.[9]

In 1948 U.S. exports to the Soviet bloc (including China) totaled $397 million, or about 21 percent of total free-world exports to the bloc ($1.9 billion), but only 3.1 percent of total U.S. trade. Between 1949 and 1950, U.S. exports to the bloc decreased from $145 million (9 percent of free-world exports to the bloc and 1.2 percent of total U.S. trade) to $64 million (4 percent of free-world exports to the bloc and 0.6 percent of total U.S. trade).[10]

In July 1947 the Soviet Union scuttled U.S. economic plans for Eastern Europe when it withdrew from the Marshall Plan conference in Paris. This action set off the two-pronged plan by the United States to replace the 1940 Export Control Act and seek multilateral cooperation to prevent the export of raw materials and strategic trade items[11] to the Soviet bloc.

In December 1947 the United States decided to institute a "postwar security export control" system of items other than munitions and atomic energy materials in response to "growing concern over shipments of strategic commodities to the Soviet bloc from both the United States and other free-world countries." The House also passed a resolution calling for controls on strategic items to the Soviet bloc.[12]

On March 1, 1948, "export control as an instrument of national security was formally instituted" when the Department of Commerce placed most exports to the Soviet bloc under mandatory licensing control. On March 24, the House adopted an amendment to the Economic Cooperation Act of 1948 (the Marshall Plan) banning export to the Soviet bloc of strategic items specifically transferred to the jurisdiction of the act.[13]

The events of 1948 served as a prelude to hearings to replace the 1940 act during the first session of Congress in 1949. Based upon the hearings, Congress made two findings:

1. Certain materials continue in short supply at home and abroad so that the quantity of U.S. exports and their distribution among importing countries affect the welfare of the domestic economy and have an important bearing upon the fulfillment of the foreign policy of the United States.
2. The unrestricted export of materials without regard to their potential military significance may affect the national security.[14]

Based on the two findings, Congress issued a three-point export control policy of "denial," as the State Department characterized it.[15] The three points are as follows:

1. to protect the domestic economy from the excessive drain of scarce materials and to reduce the inflationary impact of abnormal foreign demand;
2. to further the foreign policy of the United States to aid in fulfilling

its international responsibilities; and

3. to exercise the necessary vigilance over exports from the standpoint of their significance to the national security.[16]

In short, the Export Control Act of 1949 focused on two issues: short supply and national security. Yet the evidence indicates that by the time the act was adopted, the United States had overcome most shortages, and by February 1949 short supplies accounted for only about one-third of the export licenses processed by the Department of Commerce.[17] Although short supply was the dominant concern between 1945 and 1947, national security jumped to the fore after the Communist takeover in Czechoslovakia in March 1948.

The act gave the President broad powers to implement its provisions, including the authority to:

- "effectuate" policies by prohibiting or curtailing exports of any articles, materials, or supplies, including technical data;
- regulate the "financing, transporting, and other servicing of exports" as well as actual exports;
- delegate his power, authority, and discretion to "such departments, agencies, or officials of the Government" as he saw fit (The Department of Commerce, for one, did not seek to oversee implementation of the act, recognizing that export controls and trade promotion are bureaucratic contradictions. In the end, the Department of Commerce's Bureau of International Trade, through its Office of Export Control, was assigned the responsibility of implementing the act.);
- establish an interagency consultative mechanism to coordinate U.S. export control policy (In time, an interdepartmental consultative group was created to oversee the control list and decide licensing disputes. Two levels were formed: The Operating Committee, composed of mid-level officers from the Departments of Commerce, State, Defense, and Treasury, and the intelligence community made up the first level; the Advisory Committee on Export Policy [ACEP] was the second level. In 1961 a third level was added, the Export Control Review Board, composed of the secretaries of Commerce, State, and Defense.);
- "fully" utilize the private sector "insofar as practicable, giving consideration to the interests of small business . . . and provisions shall be made for representative trade consultations to that end";
- establish penalties for violations, with fines of not more than $10,000 or imprisonment for not more than one year; and
- enforce the provisions of the act through investigations, subpoena,

and testimony under oath.

The Positive List. The export regulations issued under the act contained a comprehensive licensing system to control the export of commodities and technical data set forth in the so-called Positive List, the forerunner to today's Commodity Control List (CCL). In March 1948 the Positive List included 2,300 separate items that required a validated export license.[18] Such items calling for a license because of national security reasons were not granted for the Sino-Soviet bloc. Items on the list for short supply and national security reasons were permitted for export to free-world destinations on a case-by-case basis, which included end-use assurances by the recipient country to guard against diversion, transshipment, or unauthorized reexport.

Items not on the Positive List were allowed to be exported to free-world destinations under a general license, but the reexport of these items to Soviet bloc destinations required a validated export license or specific authorization from Commerce.

Termination Date. The termination date for the act was June 30, 1953, or sooner upon agreement between the Congress and the President. The outbreak of war in the Korean peninsula, China's intervention, shortages of raw materials as result of the Korean War, and the successful economic recovery in Europe led to renewal of the act in 1956, 1958, 1960, 1962, and 1965 and finally to its replacement by the first Export Administration Act in 1969. By 1969, however, one of the two bases for the 1949 act--short supply--had virtually disappeared. Indeed, by 1960 there were no items controlled for short supply reasons. The most important change, however, was an intangible: the U.S. attitude toward the Soviet Union, and therefore toward national security.

The Export Administration Act of 1969

Historical Background. Cold War rhetoric began to give way to peaceful coexistence in the 1960s and finally to détente in the 1970s. As U.S. and Soviet nuclear competition leveled off, relations became less hostile, although they were also marked by less meaningful cooperation. Nonetheless, both sides concluded the Treaty on the Non-Proliferation of Nuclear Weapons (NPT) during the height of the Vietnam War. In Eastern Europe, access to West Berlin was respected by the Soviet Union; the United States, in return, tacitly accepted Soviet hegemony in Central and Eastern Europe. Both sides also acted with restraint during the 1967 Israeli-Arab conflict. "A pattern of limiting the stakes of conflict emerged," writes one scholar, "that led to the mutual desire to advance from peaceful coexistence--the maintenance of the status quo--to détente--a lessening of tension."[19]

U.S. relations toward China were also improving, although at first under considerably more secrecy. In early 1969 President Richard Nixon ordered a study of U.S.-China relations at a time when the Sino-Soviet border conflict was heating up. In 1969 the United States unilaterally relaxed certain trade and travel restrictions to China, and in early 1970 the two countries resumed talks in Warsaw. In April 1971, U.S. and Chinese Ping-Pong teams competed and set the stage for high-level bilateral talks leading to the establishment of diplomatic relations in 1978.

Congressional Hearings on the Export Control Act of 1949. The effects of détente were fully felt in Congress in May through July 1969 during its hearings on extending the Export Control Act of 1949. No one captured the mood of changing times and their effect on U.S. export control policy better than Representative Thomas L. Ashley (D-OH), a House conferee, who said:

> The Export Control Act was enacted in 1949 as a temporary measure and as a necessary weapon in the evolving cold war. At that time Western Europe, still economically weak from the ravages of the Second World War, appeared to the Congress to be in realistic danger of attack from the monolithic Sino-Soviet bloc under the leadership of Stalin; and it was further believed, comparing our industrial might with both Eastern and Western Europe at that time, that goods withheld from the Soviets by means of controls on American commodities could not be elsewhere obtained.
>
> Now, 20 years later, these underlying premises have drastically changed. . . . We have moved into a period in which the Congress should maintain a close, in-depth review of our export control laws with a view to reshaping them in light of political, economic, and technological changes taking place in Western Europe, Japan, and the Communist countries of Eastern Europe. . . . Testimony indicates . . . that we continue to unilaterally control hundreds of categories of goods on political grounds . . . that even now, 2,020 commodity categories are under control for such countries as Bulgaria, Czechoslovakia, Hungary, and the U.S.S.R., while 1,753 of these are controlled for Poland and Rumania, at the same time that COCOM has designated 552 categories for control.[20]

Ashley pointed to the United States' "compulsive tendency" to "regard the denial of trade with Communist nations as a primary instrument or weapon of the Cold War," whereas the allies did not. The allies, he said, were satisfied to use COCOM to control strategic trade but not nonstrategic trade as the United States was wont to do. He also noted that the embargo was playing into the hands of the Soviets because it enabled them to consolidate control even more. U.S. measures were "so stringent," he added, that the United States risked "political goodwill" with the allies. The embargo, he said, "has failed to shift the balance of power." Worse yet, the European allies, who were trading in nonstrategic goods, were reaping the economic benefits of that policy. Ashley noted that in 1967 free-world trade with the Soviet bloc totaled $14 billion, of which Western Europe and Japan accounted for almost $9 billion. The United States, which accounted for about 16 percent of world exports in 1967, totaled about 0.3 of the exports to Eastern Europe.[21]

Ashley concluded: "I believe that it is time to give full congressional recognition to the value in expanding trade in peaceful goods and technology with the Soviet Union and the other countries of Eastern Europe and I believe it is time our export control laws and policy implemented this objective."[22]

Ashley offered a "finding" and a "policy declaration" to the Export Control Act that would expand trade in peaceful goods and technology with all countries with which the United States had diplomatic or trade relations to foster the "sound growth and stability" of the U.S. economy and to further U.S. foreign policy objectives, except to the extent that the President determines such trade to be against the national interest.[23]

Ashley's recommendation was adopted without change in the new Export Administration Act of 1969. The State Department ruefully noted: "A new feature of the [1969] Act is congressional endorsement of a policy favoring expansion of peaceful trade with the U.S.S.R. and other Eastern European countries."[24]

Key Provisions of the 1969 Act. The 1969 act preserved intact the two findings of the 1949 act regarding short supply and national security and added two more reflecting Ashley's concerns:

- the unwarranted restriction of exports from the United States has a serious adverse effect on our balance of payments; and
- the uncertainty of policy toward certain categories of exports has curtailed the efforts of U.S. business in those categories to the detriment of the overall attempt to improve the trade balance of the United States.

"Economic security," in its initial manifestations, had begun the broadening of the U.S. export control beyond military matters.

The 1969 act included three other policy declarations from subsequent amendments to the 1949 act. One was the Ashley amendment to encourage trade with Communist countries. A second, proposed in 1962 by Senator Jacob Javits (R-NY), addressed problems created by the less restrictive policies of other non-Communist countries toward trade with Communist countries.[25] This policy was aimed at COCOM European members whose policies were less restrictive than those of the United States. The third, in response to Arab countries' subjecting U.S. firms to boycotts for dealing with Israel, established U.S. policy to use export controls to oppose restrictive trade practices or foreign boycotts. "This was," two scholars write, "the first amendment in the history of the Act which introduced provisions wholly outside the scope of export controls."[26]

The 1969 act had its desired effect: U.S. exports to Communist countries rose in both 1970 and 1971. Indeed, the rise in exports to the Soviet Union in 1971 was sharper than to other Soviet bloc countries. U.S. exports to the Soviet Union rose by over 12 percent in 1970 and by 40 percent for the first three quarters of 1971. By contrast, U.S. exports to the Soviet bloc countries rose by 63 percent in 1970 but only 22 percent in the first three quarters of 1971. In addition, in 1970, for the first time in twenty years, the free world sold more to Communist countries than it bought from them.[27]

The Export Administration Act of 1979

Between October 10, 1978, and May 7, 1979, the Congress held a series of hearings to amend and extend the EAA of 1969. Congress identified the following four needs for new legislation:[28]

1. Extend existing authority to regulate exports.
2. Improve the efficiency of export licensing and to provide for periodic and systematic review and revision of export control policy to ensure that controls . . . are not excessive. . . . Export licenses are subject to lengthy delays lasting months beyond the 90 day period specified in the law. Interagency review is seldom accomplished expeditiously . . . and foreign availability reviews are conducted separately by each agency, resulting in duplication of effort and unnecessary delays in processing applications.
3. . . . bring about appropriate and timely revision of the lists of goods and technology subject to export license control. . . . Three years after the [Defense Science Board] Task Force report [February 27, 1976], a critical technology approach has still to be devised and implemented.

4.   . . . foster consistency in U.S. export control policy and closer
cooperation with allies. Uncertainty over U.S. policy toward
the use of export controls for foreign policy purposes has
discouraged potential exports and tarnished the reputation of
U.S. exporters as reliable suppliers to foreign countries.

The "overall" intent of the new legislation, the conferees believed, was
"to reduce the regulatory impact of export controls."[29] To achieve this
goal, Congress especially addressed four areas: the use of export controls
as instruments of foreign policy, foreign availability, simplifying and
expediting export licensing procedures, and reducing reexport controls.
Of the four, "no aspect of U.S. export control policy received sharper
criticism during Committee and Subcommittee hearings than controls
maintained for foreign policy purposes."[30] Former Secretary of State Dean
Rusk, in calling for a reconsideration of the attitude of the U.S.
government toward the use of export controls for foreign policy purposes,
put it best: "I would strongly advise against a drift into self-imposed
economic isolationism by weighing trade in terms of approval or
disapproval of the institutions of other trading nations."[31]

Summary of the Incremental Nature
of U.S. Export Control Policy

The 96th Congress proceeded to add five findings and a number of
additional policy declarations. The incremental approach to the evolving
export control system was fully under way. By 1979 the evolution of U.S.
export control policy had proliferated to the following findings and policy
declarations:

Year of Act	Findings	Policies
1949	Short supply	Control short supplies
	National security	Deny strategic exports
1969	Short supply	Continue controls
	National security	Continue denial
	Controls affect balance of payments	Liberalize controls
	Controls affect trace balance	Liberalize controls

Trade with Communist countries
Harmonize allied trade policies
Use economic resources to further trade
  opportunities
Use controls to oppose boycotts

1979		
Short supply	Continue controls
National security	Continue denial
Balance of payments	Continue liberal controls
Trade balance	Continue liberal controls
Trade a fundamental right for citizens	U.S. government gives high-priority control for short supply and national security
Private sector/U.S. government cooperation	Minimize uncertainties
Fewer restrictions on world supplies, noninterference with international trade	Trade with Communist countries
Give special emphasis to militarily critical technologies	Set up interagency consultative group
Controls affect agricultural exports	Liberalize controls
	Use controls to remove unfair foreign trade practices
	Use controls as antiterrorist instruments
	Improve multilateral controls cooperation
	Use controls to oppose boycotts

The 1981 and 1985 amendments included the same findings and policy declarations of the 1979 EAA. The 1985 amendments, however, added another four findings and four policy declarations that were continued in the 1988 amendments in the 1988 Omnibus Trade Bill.

Findings	*Policies*
Special emphasis to exports for public health and environment	Controls for public health and environment reasons

Guard against Soviet technology theft	Sustain vigorous scientific enterprise
Foreign availability	Minimize dependence on imports of energy and other critical resources
Excessive dependence on energy can be harmful to U.S. and allies' security interests	Continue "no exceptions" policy brought about by Soviet shootdown of KAL-7

Conclusions

This inflationary trend in findings and policy statements leads to several conclusions:

1. Short supply controls have all but disappeared. Today the United States controls only two items for reasons of short supply: petroleum and petroleum products and unprocessed Western red cedar.
2. National security controls have remained constant since 1949, augmented in 1979 with special emphasis on militarily critical technologies and attention given to Soviet technology theft in 1985.
3. The 1969 act introduced the concept of economic security by giving emphasis to trade and payments balances. By declaring the policy to seek to remove restrictions on certain trade, the 1969 act not only broadened the objectives of the U.S. export control system but also introduced the contradictory objective of controlling exports and promoting trade. This dilemma is central to the problem facing the U.S. export control system today, and it remains unresolved.
4. Export controls have become a primary instrument of U.S. foreign policy. Since 1978 the United States has used export controls to influence the behavior of certain countries in regard to human rights (Uganda, Soviet Union), military aggression (Argentina during the Falklands-Malvinas crisis and the Soviet Union for its invasion of Afghanistan), hostage-taking (Iran), terrorism (Iraq, South Yemen, Libya), and racial segregation (South Africa). Products that have been subject to U.S. export controls range from foodstuffs to stuffed animals and blue jeans (part of the U.S. embargo of the 1980 Olympics in Moscow).
5. The 1979 act called for better cooperation between the U.S. government and the private sector, a policy that remains largely unimplemented, as will be seen.

6. The integration of the Commodity Control List and the Militarily Critical Technologies List (MCTL) called for by the 1985 amendments has not occurred.
7. Despite the increasing attention given to foreign availability since the 1979 act, it is still one of the most controversial export control policies today, and one of the least understood.
8. License processing has improved significantly, but the volume remains extremely high because of the lengthy and complex control lists.
9. Reexport controls remain a highly contentious issue with industry, friends, and allies.

Structures

Office of Munitions Control

The Office of Munitions Control is located in the State Department's Politico-Military Bureau. OMC is responsible for discharging the functions of the secretary of state in controlling commercial export of defense articles and services. OMC administers the Munitions List by a licensing process that has come under considerable criticism in the past few years.

OMC is the smallest of the three licensing agencies. According to FY-89 figures, its miniscule budget of $2.1 million provides for about thirty-five persons, including roughly a dozen licensing officers (compare that to Commerce's 554 persons and a budget of $40 million, or DOD's 135 people and nearly $6 million).

The Bureau of Export Administration

Perhaps the most significant *structural* change introduced by the 1985 amendments was the establishment of the Bureau of Export Administration (BXA). BXA was an attempt by Senator Garn to separate Commerce's export control function from its trade promotion function. Because of departmental resistance and budgeting problems, however, it took nearly two years for BXA to come into formal existance on October 1, 1987. Today, BXA has 554 persons and a budget of $40.1 million to process nearly 100,000 licenses.

The Defense Technology Security Administration

The Department of Defense had a similar idea. On January 17, 1984, Secretary of Defense Caspar Weinberger approved a proposal to establish a technology security office in DOD that would, for all intents and purposes, provide Defense with its own in-house expertise on dual-use and arms export control matters. The proposed office was as much the result of an internal power struggle between the policy and the research and engineering departments as it was to provide Defense with a key interagency player with equal status to the Commerce Department and the well-established OMC.

In 1986 the Defense Technology Security Administration (DTSA) was established to coordinate the various agencies within DOD and to expedite interagency-referred licenses. In time it became a meaner, leaner version of BXA. Within four years, DTSA grew from four to 135 persons, and its budget grew to nearly $6 million in FY-89.

Today, BXA and DTSA are electronically connected by computer, but OMC remains outside the loop. Cases referred to DTSA from State (munitions) or Commerce (dual-use) invariably take time because DTSA itself must refer licenses, where appropriate, to, among others, the National Security Agency (NSA), Defense Intelligence Agency (DIA), and the military services. As we shall see, when cases get caught in the interagency process, regardless of where they are referred, delay becomes the rule rather than the exception.

DTSA, to be sure, symbolizes the lack of trust over technical assessments and technology transfer policy among Defense, State, and Commerce. It also duplicates in large measure the functions of the Departments of Commerce and State.

The U.S. Control Lists

The evolution of the U.S. national security export control system is embodied in its control lists, arguably the most complex, lengthy, and controversial lists among the COCOM member states. The U.S. control list regime consists of the U.S. Munitions List (USML) administered by the Department of State, the Commodity Control List administered by the Department of Commerce, and the Nuclear Referral List (NRL) administered by the Departments of Commerce and Energy. The Department of Defense is responsible for compiling still a fourth list, the Militarily Critical Technologies List, which, though not formally a "control" list, is at best treated as one and is at worst, on the verge of competing with the CCL as the authoritative dual-use technologies control list.

The U.S. Munitions List

Section 38 of the Arms Export Control Act of 1976 contains the current statutory authority for regulating commercial arms exports, the International Trafficking in Arms Regulations. In 1976 the President delegated the authority to license the export of commercial arms to the secretaries of state pursuant to Executive Order 11958. The ITAR defines the items that make up the USML. These items are designated with the concurrence of the secretaries of state and defense. Defense is responsible for identifying those items or categories considered as defense articles and services.

The USML is composed of the following categories: firearms, artillery projectors, ammunition, launch vehicles, guided missiles, ballistic missiles, rockets, torpedoes, bombs, mines, explosives, vessels of war, tanks, aircraft, spacecraft, military training equipment, protective personnel equipment, military and space electronics, fire control, range finders, optical and guidance and control equipment, auxiliary military equipment, toxicological agents and equipment, nuclear weapons design and test equipment, defense services, and submersible vessels.

The USML is a relatively short document; it is fewer than ten pages long. By contrast, Commerce's CCL is 162 pages.

The issue that generates the most complaints by U.S. exporters is commodity jurisdiction disputes between Commerce and State.[32] A commodity jurisdiction procedure is used if the U.S. government is unsure whether an article is on the Munitions List. The procedure entails consultations among the Departments of State, Commerce, and Defense and involves lengthy delays in license processing and referral.

In order to initiate a commodity jurisdiction determination, an exporter must submit a request supported by the exporter's own evidence (brochures or specifications relating to the item) to OMC. OMC will refer the exporter's request for commodity determination to the other agencies *if* there is doubt whether the commodity is controlled by the USML or CCL. Licensing delays may result if there is a disagreement between the departments. Commodity jurisdiction requests, then, are referred to Defense or Commerce only if a question arises. Otherwise, OMC declares the commodity under its jurisdiction.

It is, to quote an old cliché, easier said than done, as the following case study illustrates. In 1984 the Department of Commerce approved a license for the export of a $1.2 million Combined Acceleration Vibration Climatic Test System (CAVCTS), or, as it is commonly known, a "shake and bake" device. The simulation device allows payloads to be accelerated at the gravitational pull of the earth, thereby submitting the components of vehicles to the heat and stresses of reentry. The device was designed for

India's Defense Research and Development Laboratory. The license was issued in May 1985, but for reasons of its own, India failed to request shipment of the test system within the two-year period for which licenses were valid (licenses are now valid for three years).

In August 1987 the U.S. firms resubmitted the license application, only this time the license faced an obstacle not present in 1985: the Missile Technology Control Regime (MTCR), a nontreaty, nonbinding arrangement entered into by seven major economic powers in April 1987 to control the export of nuclear-capable equipment and technologies (see Chapter 3 for a more detailed discussion of the MTCR). Opponents of the export argued that the "shake and bake" device would contribute to India's missile program. Proponents argued that the device in question was not on the MTCR control list (a subset of both the U.S. Munitions and Commodity Control Lists, and therefore licensed by State or Commerce) and, further, that the sale was protected by contract sanctity. (In order for the contract to be rescinded, the President is required to find that the export will cause a "breach of the peace," a stringent condition I and others added to the EAA in 1985 after the fiasco of the Soviet natural gas pipeline controls severely hurt our credibility as suppliers and caused European producers to begin "designing out" U.S. components from their products.)

In the last days of the Reagan Administration, the argument shifted from policy considerations to commodity jurisdiction grounds, a much neater and less controversial way to deny the export. Opponents argued that although the test system's force level was well within the 22,500-pound limit set by the MTCR, there was particular concern over the system's simultaneous multiple testing capability.[33] Lost in this argument was note of a more powerful device (35,000 pounds), that had been shipped to India previously as a dual-use export approved by Commerce. It took OMC nearly six months to determine that the device was a munitions item and not exportable to India.

The case, therefore, took nearly five years to decide, and was resolved only after a Houdini-like gambit shifted the item from one list to the other. The merits of the case--the force of the device itself, whether or not India intended to divert the device from its space program to its nuclear missile program, and the applicability of the MTCR itself--seem to have disappeared in the process.

The Commodity Control List

The 1988 version of the Export Administration regulations contains 750 pages. The implementing regulations alone total 588 pages. The

Commodity Control List is 162 pages with over 200 entries divided into ten categories, not including nearly thirty categories controlled unilaterally for national security reasons. Not surprisingly, the CCL has been characterized by industry as "impenetrable" and "obfuscatory." One expert writes: "In a real sense the CCL gives meaning and substance to congressional intent. It is the flesh on the legislative skeleton. Its evolution is a constant series of deletions, additions, and amendments. . . . Since 1981 the momentum has been to increase list coverage. . . . Overly extensive coverage may well decrease business's voluntary compliance and, ultimately, sap the very legitimacy of the system."[34]

The Nuclear Referral List

The United States was the first nuclear weapon state and is still considered the leader in nuclear technology. Under the Atomic Energy Act of 1946, the United States instituted export controls on sharing nuclear information and embargoed the export or import of any fissionable material. The Atomic Energy Act of 1954 provided for sharing the benefits of nuclear energy in exchange for the peaceful use of atomic energy by recipient countries. In 1957 the International Atomic Energy Agency (IAEA) was established to safeguard items of U.S. origin. In 1970 the Treaty on the Non-Proliferation of Nuclear Weapons entered into force, among other reasons, in order to safeguard all nuclear materials in NPT member territories. This legal structure was expanded further in 1978 with the enactment of the Nuclear Non-Proliferation Act (NNPA). The NNPA, the NPT, and the IAEA safeguards remain today the key legal instruments for advancing the nonproliferation interests of the United States.

The Departments of Energy and Commerce share responsibility for the export of nuclear-related equipment and technology. Energy's Nuclear Regulatory Commission (NRC) is responsible for licensing the export of nuclear reactors or fuel after interagency review by the Departments of Energy, State, Defense, and Commerce and the Arms Control and Disarmament Agency (ACDA) have determined that the proposed exports "will not be inimical to the common defense and security."[35] (This part of the nuclear export control system is outside the focus of this book.)

Section 309(c) of the NNPA requires the President to publish procedures regarding control by the Department of Commerce over the export of those items listed in the CCL and identified as "nuclear nonproliferation." These commodities are subject to validated licensing and are known as the Nuclear Referral List. Controls also exist for exports of technology to foreign maritime nuclear propulsion projects and certain other technical data.

The Subgroup on Nuclear Export Coordination. Proposed exports of commodities on the Nuclear Referral List are referred to a special interagency committee, the Subgroup on Nuclear Export Coordination (SNEC), which is chaired by the State Department. The SNEC is empowered to recommend action on the proposed license, including end-use certification based on government-to-government or private assurances concerning the item's end-use and guarantees of access to verify that use.

The Country List. The Commodity Control List indicates the countries to which validated licenses are required. Some commodities are controlled for nuclear reasons to all country groups, and in certain instances to Canada. Supplement No. 2 to Part 778 of the Export Administration Regulations lists the countries that are party to the Nuclear Non-Proliferation Treaty, the Treaty for the Prohibition of Nuclear Weapons in Latin America (Treaty of Tlatelolco), or both, and for whom nuclear controls apply in particular. Countries that are not members of the NNPT or Treaty of Tlatelolco and therefore present special problems for proposed exports of items on the Nuclear Referral List include Argentina, Brazil, China, India, Israel, Pakistan, and South Africa. The U.S.-Chinese nuclear energy agreement was suspended on June 5, 1989, as a result of the Tiananmen Square incident.

The Militarily Critical Technologies List

The 1979 Export Administration Act, more than any other revision, made the Department of Defense a major player in the U.S. export control system. For example, it authorized Defense to establish its own guidelines for evaluating technologies and their export. Defense administered the Militarily Critical Technologies List, a compendium of dual-use technologies and munitions items with special emphasis on:

1. design and manufacturing know-how;
2. keystone manufacturing, inspection, and test equipment;
3. goods accompanied by sophisticated operation, application, or maintenance know-how; and
4. keystone equipment that would give insight into the design or manufacture of U.S. military systems.

The Relationship of the MCTL to the CCL and USML

How does the MCTL relate to the USML and CCL? According to DTSA, the MCTL is "not a control document"; it is a technical reference and source document to support the development of export control policy and specific proposals on the COCOM International List, the CCL, and the ITAR. The MCTL also has a set of supporting documents--technical analyses, intelligence assessments, industry comments, and reviews from technical experts--that provide information on the military significance, foreign capabilities, transfer mechanisms, and technical details for the nearly 600 technologies organized under twenty categories that make up the list. Internally, the MCTL provides information to DOD licensing officers on items controlled by the CCL and USML.

The MCTL is a classified document totaling over 800 pages. At times, portions are declassified for a number of reasons, primarily to share information with the network of private-sector "technical advisory committees" that advise the U.S. government through the Department of Commerce. The MCTL, as we shall see below in the case study of decontrol of certain personal computers, can cut both ways.

The Defense Department jealously guards its authority over the MCTL, and in the past has attempted, without success, to give it the status of the CCL. COCOM, which already is critical of the United States' lengthy control lists, continues to guard against efforts by the Defense Department to use the MCTL to drive the list review process and to increase the number of items to be controlled multilaterally.

The Licensing Maze

Time is money. And nowhere is more money allegedly lost by exporters than in the U.S. export licensing systems. In its 1987 study, the NAS found that "licensing delays and uncertainties remain a problem for a significant percentage of export transactions. . . .Shipping delays impose immediate financial costs on the exporter as well as a longer-term cost in customer confidence."[36]

The General Accounting Office (GAO) report regarding DTSA's role in reviewing export license cases recommended that the agencies responsible for administering the export control system should "amend the Export Administration Regulations to clearly state U.S. policy and prescribe procedures for the use of commonly used conditions for approving export licenses, especially no resale and no transfer (reexports)."[37]

In discussion with the private sector in preparation for introducing the OSTT Bill, it became clear that the complexities of applying for an export license and tracking the license through the system had spawned a lucrative consulting business. This group of consultants is the most opposed to export control reform.

It should be clear by now that several executive branch agencies have a responsibility for reviewing export control licenses, including the Departments of State, Commerce, Defense, Treasury, and Energy; ACDA; NSA; CIA; NASA; and U.S. Customs, to name the obvious ones. But the licensing process itself must be appreciated to understand why it has given rise to a profitable industry devoted to interpreting export control arcana. Let us look at OMC and Commerce's licensing systems, and DTSA's role in both.

OMC Licensing Maze

As Table 1.2 shows, in 1988, OMC received 54,502 license applications. Of those it approved 49,755, returned 4,051 without action, and denied 660. Approximately 80 percent of the licenses were routinely processed. The remaining 20 percent were referred to the Department of Defense, ACDA, NASA, or the Department of Energy, depending on the export involved.

According to one specialist, "there are no standard staffing patterns" for licenses referred for interagency review.[38] A recommendation to deny by any one referral agency is generally sufficient for denial. As this specialist describes the process,

> If the veto is cast by the cognizant regional bureau in State it will be denied on foreign policy ground even though the other reviewing parties may have expressed no objections. If, however, the recommended denial stems from one of the functional bureaus or ACDA, OMC will consult the regional bureau concerned to see if it will concur in the denial or attempt to resolve the difference by escalating the decision to the policy level if necessary. . . . State usually accedes to Defense's recommendations to deny if they are adequately justified on national security grounds.[39]

In recent years, the Department of Defense has recommended denial of fewer than 10 percent of the nearly 10,000 licenses referred to it. The denial percentage, however, has grown steadily since the early 1970s, when in a typical year only 1 or 2 percent were denied overall. Industry, not surprisingly, considers Defense's steadily increasing denials as *one* important factor in the decline of defense exports (see Chapter 4).

TABLE 1.2
OMC Licensing Figures, 1983-1988 (in billions of U.S. dollars)

Fiscal Year	Total Licenses	Authorized Exports	Actual Exports
1983	40,572	8.7	4.0
1984	46,441	12.7	3.8
1985	44,848	9.9	2.3
1986	49,171	25.1	4.2
1987	53,966	27.7	5.6
1988	54,502	30.2	8.1

Sources: Data for 1983-1985: U.S. General Accounting Office. *Report on Arms Export Licensing at the Department of State, 1987*. GAO reports that OMC approves about 90 percent of all licenses, denies 2 percent and returns 8 percent without action. Data for 1986-1988: OMC. Licenses reviewed as part of this report were valid for two years. Licenses are now valid for three years.

In March 1987 the General Accounting Office reviewed OMC's licensing activities and procedures at the request of Congress.[40] The study found four serious problems with OMC's license application review process and exporters' compliance with administrative and reporting requirements:

1. OMC did not routinely check export license application data and information and rarely requested U.S. embassies' assistance in verifying the bona fides of the purchaser or other foreign parties to the sale.
2. OMC's facilities and automation capabilities were not sufficient to provide much assistance to licensing officers during their reviews.
3. OMC did not have adequate systems and procedures to ensure that exporters comply with administrative requirements.
4. OMC understated the values on authorized arms exports and exports actually made in its reports.

Two years later, GAO credits OMC with making some progress in all four areas but remains critical of OMC's slow pace in improving its electronic capabilities, particularly computerization of the licensing system.

Commerce Licensing Maze

The number of licenses processed by Commerce annually is staggering. In 1988 alone, for example, Commerce processed 96,593 license applications, approved 90,650, returned 4,941 without action, and denied 555. Of the total approved, 98.5 percent were processed in fewer than 120 days. Of the nearly 1,000 licenses with a value of over $1.5 billion that took over four months to process, all required special handling. A breakdown of those reveals the following reasons for the delay:

Reasons for Delay	Licenses (%)
Interagency disputes, East-West licenses	25-30
Prelicense checks by Commerce	20
Waiting for government-to-government assurances	25-30
"Black hole" cases (no one doing anything, foreign policy controls, China, Soviet bloc, system paralysis, cases too complicated for current system)	25-30

Licensing time lines clearly contribute to the complexities of processing export license applications. An analysis of Section 10 of the EAA, which specifies procedures and time lines, shows that licenses may be processed in as little as ten days or as long as infinity. Section 10 also explains the rise of a lucrative export-license consulting business.

Type of License	Processing Time
Sec. 10(b)	10 days for initial screening
Sec. 10(d)	20 days for referral to other agencies
Sec. 10(e)	40 days (Add 20 days to 10(d))
Sec. 10(e)(2)(A)	40 days for approval/denial
Sec. 10(g)(2)(C)	80 days for DOD/Presidential action
Sec. 10(f)(2)(A)	90 days
Sec. 10(f)(1)	120 days
Sec. 10(f)(3)	150 days
Sec. 10(h)	160 days for multilateral controls
Sec. 10(f)(4) and 10(h) subject to 10(i)(3)	No time limit

To cut through the maze of licensing time lines, Commerce has adopted the following informal in-house rules:

Type of Licence	Processing Time
Not requiring referral	60 days
Requiring referral	120 days
Submitted to COCOM	160 days

In addition to mastering the interagency process and licensing time lines, an exporter must also be familiar with the diverse number of licenses required for exports. The 1988 EAA provides for four types of validated licenses: individual, project, distribution, and service supply. In addition there are about twenty-five general license provisions in the Export Administration Regulations, including G-DEST, G-COM, CGC, C-CEU, CFW, and G-COCOM, and others to identify transactions that are not really exports, such as GIT, BAGGAGE, G-FTZ, SHIP STORES, PLANE STORES, CREW, RCS, GTF- U.S., GLR, GATS, G-NNR, GTDA, GTDR, and GTE.

DOD's Role in Licensing Decisions[41]

We have noted that during the 1983-1985 debate to expand DOD's authority to review licenses West-West, DOD based its argument on its ability to spot potential diverters using its own technical and intelligence resources.

In June 1989 Congress asked the General Accounting Office to examine the roles of the Departments of Commerce and Defense in export licensing. The study was also undertaken in anticipation of DOD's request for an increase in DTSA's budget from $5.7 million in FY-89 to $10.6 million for FY-90. The GAO's findings, with which DOD "generally concurred," are interesting.

First, the GAO found that DTSA's recommendations "generally agreed with Commerce's ultimate licensing decision following interagency review" on 90 percent of the cases reviewed by the GAO. Nonetheless, Commerce denied seventy-one cases approved by DTSA based on Commerce's own concern about diversion or Department of Energy concerns about unacceptable nuclear end-uses. Second, the GAO found that DTSA's influence was greatest in the review of West-East cases. Commerce changed its initial licensing decision on 36 percent of the cases based on DTSA's recommendation. Third, and a finding related to the 1985 decision, DTSA's reviews and recommendations regarding West-West licensing decisions changed Commerce's decision *on only 4 percent of the cases reviewed by the GAO.* Finally, the GAO found that the number of cases reviewed by DTSA decreased from nearly 21,000 in 1986 to about 11,000 in 1988, casting further doubt on DTSA's request for budgetary increases.

Next to OMC, the delays caused by SNEC review have drawn the most criticism by industry. Section 309(c) of the Nuclear Non-Proliferation Act provides for a thirty-day review period of licenses with an additional thirty days granted if the review cannot be completed within the initial period. According to industry sources, it is not uncommon for the SNEC to take over six months to review licenses, and industry representatives told of licenses that took over a year to process.

Critiques of the Export Control System

In 1967, two years before the Export Control Act of 1949 was to be replaced by the 1969 act, two experts wrote:

> The time has come to re-examine seriously ... the Export Control Act. . . . The question must be asked: Can methods of export control which were adopted initially as a temporary wartime expedient serve adequately for the indefinite future? We must also ask whether, if export licensing has in fact become a permanent part of our economic and legal order, it is wise to divide the main burden of administering it between three different departments of the Government. Closely related to the question of methods of control is the question of criteria for granting or denying license applications; these criteria must be analyzed in order to determine whether they in fact promote the aims of national security and foreign policy which the Export Control Act affirms. . . . Our system of export controls needs a drastic revision. [42]

Indeed, the saying "The more things change, the more they stay the same" comes readily to mind; as does Yogi Berra's immortal quip, "It's déjà vu all over again." As reauthorization of the EAA approached in September 1990, one could only conclude that the system still "needs a drastic revision," as the following critiques demonstrate.

Industry Criticism of Munitions Controls

In 1989, industry representatives appeared several times before Congressional committees with oversight of the AECA and other defense-related areas. In discussions of OMC's role, the criticisms were severe. The following are selected comments from those Congressional hearings:

> [After complimenting OMC for certain improvements, this witness continued]: The policies on which OMC's practices and procedures are based are excessively restrictive and burdensome. . . . The licensing process at OMC is inefficient and time

consuming. . . . The [licensing] process is . . . unpredictable.
Meanwhile, U.S. companies must compete with foreign suppliers
who, with the active support of their governments, sell defense
[articles] throughout the free world. . . . This contributes to the
image of U.S. manufacturers as unreliable suppliers.[43]

The U.S. defense export policies established well over forty years
ago are not responsive today, to meet the challenges of the
global marketplace. The current system was originally designed
immediately after World War II, at a time when the United States
was technologically and militarily without equal throughout the
world. Today this is no longer realistic. In today's world we
must realize that national security is comprised of many facets,
which include the U.S. industrial base as well as military
superiority.[44]

One industry fact sheet sent to my office had this to say about OMC:

Issue: Inadequate management resources and procedures have
resulted in a slow, inefficient and burdensome [munitions]
licensing system which is contrary to the best interests of U.S.
foreign and fiscal policy. Burdensome policies exacerbate the
situations. Revisions to the regulations implementing recent
legislative changes have added further burdens.[45]

Finally, one industry consultant wrote the following complaint:

Many exporters are of the view that (a) there is needless
duplication in two export licensing systems, (b) jurisdictional
issues (i.e., whether a product should be maintained on the ITAR
or CCL) would diminish if there were a single agency
responsible, and (c) the exporting community, especially in
defense-related products and technology, must have a licensing
system that works with maximum efficiency.[46]

Critiques of the EAA

BXA has made impressive strides in the past several years in
regularizing and streamlining the export control process. Nonetheless,
BXA, along with OMC, has attracted its share of critics, including the
National Academy of Sciences, the Congress, and two important
private-sector entities--the President's Export Council Subcommittee on

Export Administration, and the Business Roundtable.

The National Academy of Sciences. This group's landmark 1987 study made two basic recommendations with seventeen corollary prescriptions. Following is a selected sample of the NAS findings:

- The administrative structures established by the executive branch have not proven effective in resolving in a coherent and timely fashion the frequent policy differences that occur among these agencies on matters relating to national security export controls.
- U.S. national security export controls are not generally perceived as rational, credible, and predictable by many of the nations and commercial interests whose active cooperation is required for an effective system. The [NAS] concurs with this judgment.
- National security export controls impede the ability of U.S. companies to compete in world markets.
- There is a need for high-level industry input in the formulation of national security export control policy.
- The extraterritorial reach of U.S. controls damages allied relations and disadvantages U.S. exporters.[47]

Congress. Congress modified the EAA by passing the Omnibus Trade and Competitiveness Act of 1988 (OTCA), which reduced export disincentives and strengthened export enforcement. The latter provision was partly in response to the diversion of controlled machine tools to the Soviet Union by Toshiba and Kongsberg (see Chapter 5). The 1988 trade bill reduced or eliminated some licensing requirements for exports to COCOM countries and for goods that could be exported to the People's Republic of China (PRC) under the green line (see Chapter 3) called for the reduction of the CCL, strengthened the concept of foreign availability, expanded trade with China by authorizing a distribution license (suspended after the Tiananmen massacre), limited the dispute resolution mechanism to national security (not foreign policy) considerations, and provided for stronger enforcement of U.S. and COCOM controls. It took the Department of Commerce over a year to draft and publish the bulk of the regulations that were mandated by the new law--including two new general licenses for exports to COCOM and the free world and an increase from 10 to 25 percent in the proportion of U.S. parts and components that would bring a product under controls for reexport purposes.

The one regulation that has not been published as this is written is also one of the most controversial: the definition of a supercomputer. That case illustrates two points: (1) the extent to which the system is gridlocked by a contentious interagency process, and (2) considerations of extraterritorial aspects of U.S. reexport controls. Foreign manufacturers and their governments are concerned with U.S. restrictions on items manufactured abroad with U.S. parts and components; U.S. parts and components manufacturers are concerned with foreign manufacturers' designing out U.S. parts and components. The computer industry as a whole is concerned with a definition of supercomputers that would potentially apply controls to desktop models.

Since the establishment of COCOM in 1950s, the United States has been the only government to apply reexport controls on items of U.S. origin exported by other countries. In the early 1950s, this control was known as the U.S. "nonfrustration" control. According to the State Department, "To prevent the frustration of the United States export control policy and program, the Department of Commerce has followed since 1949 the general practice of refusing to license exports of certain strategic commodities to friendly countries where the country of destination does not control shipments of those commodities to the Soviet bloc."[48]

Section 2414 of the OTCA called for Commerce to define supercomputers for the purpose of reexport controls by late November 1988. In 1990 an interagency working group arrived at such a definition, which requires OMB approval before it is implemented. Once a definition is reached, private-sector groups affected by the decision who wish to make their views known have an additional six months to comment. At that pace, the final definition would have coincided with the expiration of the EAA on September 30, 1990, nearly two years after the trade bill was enacted, but was suspended by reauthorization legislation.

Sections 5(a)(4) and (5) of the EAA generally prohibit imposition of national security controls on reexports to COCOM or 5(k) countries (non-COCOM members that have adopted equivalent control regimes) and reexports of foreign manufactured goods that incorporate 25 percent or less of U.S. parts and components. Supercomputers, however, fall outside these provisions because of their military significance. In this case, Commerce retains the authority to control the reexport of supercomputers because of both national security and nuclear nonproliferation considerations. Current rules, however, impose reexport requirements on supercomputers without defining these systems. A definition became necessary because Commerce decided to retain reexport control.

Why is it taking so long for Commerce to arrive at a definition? One reason is the variety of computers available today with the potential to qualify as "supercomputers." The Department of Defense and the intelligence community have pressed a definition that applies to all mainframe computers and certain desktops. Another reason is that Commerce is sailing in uncharted waters. The administration has attracted criticism from the supercomputer industry because of Commerce's decision to use several "measures of performance" as the basis for defining the systems. The computer industry agreed that using the measure of "theoretical peak performance" (TPP) is appropriate.

Specifically, Commerce proposes to define a supercomputer using million "floating point operations per second" (MFLOP). By this definition, the regulations would not allow the export of supercomputers capable of performing more than 300 MFLOPs except to countries in the Organization for Economic Cooperation and Development (OECD). The threshold for non-OECD countries is set at 150 MFLOPs, and that for reexport of supercomputers is an even lower 100 MFLOPs.

The computer industry argues that technology is moving so rapidly that the definition of a supercomputer promises to become a moving target, with changes occurring on an annual basis. For example, the availability of RISC microprocessor chips such as the Intel chip, i860, "has significant implications for the supercomputer definition and raises questions about the treatment of general purpose equipment such as workstations and personal computers."[49] In addition, European computer manufacturers are reportedly working on 500-MFLOP desktop computers, Japanese manufacturers on 22 to 23 gigaflops (1 gigaflop is equivalent to 1 billion floating points per second).

Japan also potentially stands to benefit from the low threshold. Currently, the United States is engaged in a controversy with Japan over Japan's alleged refusal to buy supercomputers from U.S. firms. The new definition could allow the Japanese government to argue that there is not a government procurement problem for supercomputers as Japan does purchase computers not generally recognized as supercomputers but that could be designated as such under the proposed new definition. Not surprisingly, the U.S. computer industry has vowed to "holler blue murder" if and when the supercomputer definition is formally adopted.[50]

The OTCA also provided for a second NAS study of the U.S. national security export control system. Unfortunately, it took over nine months rather than the statutory sixty days for the Departments of State, Commerce, and Defense to set up the parameters for the study. The study was intended as one input to the next EAA reauthorization, but because it will take eighteen months, it will not be finished until after the next revision is completed, unless Congress postpones the expiration date.

President's Export Council Subcommittee on Export Administration. The private sector has never been accorded the attention and opportunity for input to the U.S. and COCOM export control systems that other COCOM countries give their industry. Therefore, it should come as no surprise that the private sector's views of the U.S. and COCOM systems are often critical.

The President's Export Council is a national advisory committee established by executive order to advise the President on matters related to U.S. international trade. Its membership includes both public- and private-sector representatives. The council is composed of subcommittees responsible for trade expansion, foreign trade practices, U.S. trade laws, international competitiveness, and export administration. The Subcommittee on Export Administration is the only separately chartered subcommittee. The membership is drawn not only from the parent council but also from the government and from private firms that produce goods and technical data subject to export controls.

The 1988 and 1989 reports to the President are fertile ground for judging the private sector's views of the U.S. export control system. Among the numerous findings and recommendations contained in the PEC's 1988 report,[51] one stands out. In a summary made by eight participating organizations (PEC, National Association of Manufacturers, Business Higher Education Forum, American Electronics Association, Committee on Economic Development, Chamber of Commerce, Council on Competitiveness, and the Business Roundtable), seven recommended that U.S. export control policy be revised and six of the eight recommended reduction of the budget deficit. In short, the report singled out export controls as a major problem area along with more visible ones like the budget deficit.

In the letter of transmission from the chairman of the PECSEA to Commerce Secretary Robert Mosbacher, the PECSEA wrote the following about its aims for 1989:

> The four goals were: Establish a dialogue between industry and government, simplify export controls and reduce the burden for U.S. business, reduce unilateral controls and strengthen multilateral controls, *and work toward a comprehensive structural reform of the export control system* [my emphasis]. . . . There are some significant problems to be solved in order to advance the U.S. export position, particularly for high-technology products. There are [commodity] jurisdictional issues between Commerce, State, and Defense, especially relative to so-called "dual-use" products. These are essentially U.S. internally resolvable problems. As long as these issues lie in a somewhat amorphous state of solution, it hampers our ability to come to firm grips on the export issue with our fellow COCOM members and other nations in the West who are becoming stronger competitors.
>
> The jurisdictional issue is reflected in another problem area: the export license dispute resolution procedures. The problem of "streamlining" the U.S. Government export controls interagency

review and dispute process has been attacked by prior administrations but when all is said and done, the results of the process, as viewed by industry, have fallen short.

The clarion call for structural reform of the U.S. export control system is still being heard. . . . Looking over the last year's PECSEA activity, less than 25 percent of the issues undertaken for study were initiated at the government's request. Over 75 percent were issues which the industry members believed were worthy of study because they felt these issues hindered the export administration process. . . . a more pro-active role by the government in bringing issues to the PECSEA would be helpful.[52]

The Business Roundtable. The Business Roundtable is an association of more than 200 leading companies whose chief executives focus on and act on public policy issues. In anticipation of EAA reauthorization, the Roundtable prepared a lengthy in-depth proposal that was submitted to, among others, the Congress. The proposal contains seventeen discrete recommendations to improve the EAA, inclulding the following points:

- despite important legislative changes in 1985 and 1988, the export control system is still not properly balancing [military security, economic strength, and technological leadership].
- The system has failed . . . to keep pace with dynamic economic, political, and technological developments.
- U.S. technological leadership that once could be taken for granted has eroded in many critical areas. U.S. companies now face competition from the newly industrialized countries of Asia and Latin America, which do not subject their producers to the same type of export controls as in the United States. U.S. companies also face increased competition from [EC-92].
- By failing to keep pace with these developments, the export control system continues to impose unnecessary burdens on U.S. exporters, particularly those in the high technology area. U.S. exporters must contend with a complex and often inconsistent set of national export controls. The system also continues to create uncertainties among customers regarding the ability of U.S. firms to supply products and technologies in a timely, competitive manner. As a result, it encourages foreign customers to "design out" U.S. products and technologies.
- Current export restrictions often are unnecessary to the realization of military security. . . . As a result, when export controls undermine the commercial vitality of U.S. high technology industries, they also

damage military security.[53]

Among the specific recommendations, the Roundtable singled out harmonizing the control lists, creating a "license-free" zone, improving the foreign availability process, expanding COCOM, streamlining the control lists, improving the U.S. licensing system, improving the interagency dispute resolution process, upgrading personnel and equipment at BXA and OMC, removing unnecessary foreign policy controls, terminating certain unilateral national security controls, and restricting retroactive controls.

Summary

In many respects, the export control process is reminiscent of the not-so-flattering saying that a camel is a horse designed by committee. The key to an efficient, rational, and predictable export control system for the 1990s lies in its ability to develop and administer coherent policies. An organization without coherent policies becomes dysfunctional; policies without an efficient coordinating and implementing authority become diffuse and uncertain.

The current system will fail to meet that standard in the years to come in several respects. Consider, for example, the following characteristics:

1. a trifurcated control list, which assigns oversight of one type of technology to the Department of Commerce (dual-use), another to the State Department (munitions), splits another between the Departments of Energy and Commerce (nuclear), and leaves all dependent on the technical findings by the Department of Defense;

2. a munitions licensing system that assigns licensing and foreign policy oversight to the State Department and technical oversight and a veto to the Department of Defense, ACDA, and other agencies, thereby ensuring licensing gridlock;

3. two licensing systems, but the absence of a mechanism to resolve the contentious issue called "commodity jurisdiction," whereby certain technologies are claimed by both licensing systems;

4. an executive branch referral system that could involve as few as one agency or department and as many as a dozen (the China satellite launch decision, for example, involved over twenty agencies and departments) but does not establish a clear line of decision and policymaking authority between the three key line agencies--the Departments of State, Commerce, and Defense;

5. a system that guarantees interagency conflict but does not provide an effective dispute resolution mechanism to resolve issues;

6. a system with nearly 750 people collectively in BXA, OMC, and DTSA with a combined budget of $48 million to process 150,057 licenses, as of 1988, of which only about 1 percent require special attention by either licensing system; and

7. a system that builds in mutually incompatible missions within the principal agencies responsible for carrying out export control policies, rendering them unable to balance--much less manage--the natural tension between national and economic security interests. (The Department of Commerce is commercially unable to balance and manage trade promotion and trade controls. The Department of Defense is militarily unable to strike a balance between arms cooperation and technology transfer programs. The Department of State is diplomatically unable to balance foreign policy goals and technology transfer programs. The National Security Council staff is conceptually unable to balance policy coordination and policy leadership. U.S. Customs and Commerce cannot agree on enforcement cooperation abroad.)

And the entire system is heading into a collision course with COCOM.

Notes

1. "Foreign Assets Control Regulations for the Exporting Community," U.S. Department of the Treasury, October 1988.

2. Joseph P. Smaldone, "U.S. Commercial Arms Exports: Policy, Process, and Patterns," in Louscher and Salomone (eds.), *Marketing Security Assistance* (Toronto: D. C. Heath and Co., 1987), pp. 185-214.

3. As this is being written, the Department of State has created the new Center for Defense Trade, which integrates the Office of Munitions Control and Strategic Technologies Affairs. OMC has been renamed "Office of Defense Trade Controls" but has not changed its licensing functions at all. Because it is the more familiar term, I have retained OMC throughout this paper.

4. "Excerpts from a Lawyer's Guide to International Business Transactions," in Stanley D. Metzger, *Law of International Trade: Documents and Readings*, Vol. 2 (Washington, D.C.: Lerner Law Book Company, 1966), p. 1001, and U.S. Department of State, *The Strategic Trade Control System, 1948-1956*, Ninth Report to Congress (1957) on Operations under the Mutual Defense Assistance Control Act of 1951 (the Battle Act Report), in Metzger, *Law of International Trade*, p. 1047. The Battle Act of 1951 required annual reports to the Congress. Hereafter, citations to these reports will be identified by number (or title and number) and date.

5. Harold J. Berman and John R. Garson, "United States Export Controls--Past, Present, and Future," *Columbia Law Review*, 67, 5 (May 1967), pp. 792-794, and "Excerpts from a Lawyer's Guide," in Metzger, *Law of International Trade*, p. 1001.

6. Metzger, *Law of International Trade*, p. 1001.

7. *World-Wide Enforcement of Strategic Trade Controls*, Third Battle Act Report, first half of 1953, p. 20.

8. *A Program for the Denial of Strategic Goods to the Soviet Bloc*, First Battle Act Report, 1952, p. 5.

9. Ninth Battle Act Report, 1957, in Metzger, *Law of International Trade*, pp. 1047-1048.

10. First Battle Act Report, 1952, p. 103.

11. The U.S. government defined "strategic" trade broadly as an item that would contribute significantly to Soviet war potential. Items were either of primary or secondary importance, and the underlying distinction was the "quantity" of the item available to the Soviet bloc. Primary items were considered important "in any quantity," whereas secondary items were of strategic importance if they were exported "in large quantities." (First Battle Act Report, 1952, p. 8).

12. Metzger, "Excerpts from a Lawyer's Guide," *Law of International Trade*, p. 1051.

13. Ibid., p. 1053.

14. Act of February 28, 1949, ch. 11, 63 Stat. 7, as amended, 50 U.S.C. App. Sec. 2021. Hereafter, the Export Control Act of 1949.

15. The title of the First Battle Act Report, 1952, was *A Program for the Denial of Strategic Goods to the Soviet Bloc.*

16. Export Control Act of 1949, Sec. 2022.

17. Berman and Garson, "United States Export Controls," pp. 795-796. Over the years, the United States has applied controls for short supply reasons to copper, zinc, lead, tin, aluminum, cereals, beet and cane sugar, walnut logs, bolts, hewn timber, cattle hides, and kip calfskin, and bovine leathers. Currently the United States retains short supply controls only on petroleum and petroleum products and unprocessed Western red cedar.

18. Metzger, "Excerpts from a Lawyer's Guide," *Law of International Trade*, p. 1054.

19. Robert D. Cantor, *Introduction to International Politics* (Itasca, Ill: F. E. Peacock Publishers, 1976), pp. 291-292.

20. "Supplemental Views" of Thomas L. Ashley during five days of hearings before the Subcommittee on International Trade between May 22 and July 24, 1969, in "Legislative History of the Export Administration Act of 1969," *Congressional Record*, 1969, pp. H2707-H2710.

21. Ibid., pp. 2708-2709.

22. Ibid., p. 2710.

23. Ibid.

24. Twenty-second Battle Act Report, 1969, p. 3.

25. Berman and Garson, "United States Export Controls," p. 801.

26. Ibid., p. 804.

27. Twenty-fourth Battle Act Report, 1971, pp. 5-13.

28. *Legislative History*, 96th Congress, 1st Session, 1979, Vol. 2 (St. Paul, Minn.: West Publishing Co., n.d.), pp. 1147-1197.

29. Ibid., p. 1177.

30. Ibid., p. 1152.

31. Ibid., p. 1153.

32. The information for this issue comes mainly from David Ottaway's two articles, "Bush Administration Debates Sales of Missile-Testing Device to India," *Washington Post*, May 28, 1989, and "U.S. to Bar India's Buying Missile Device," *Washington Post*, July 17, 1989.

33. Ottaway, "Bush Administration Debates Sales."

34. John R. McIntyre, "Licensing East-West High Technology Trade," in Gary K. Bertsch (ed.), *Controlling East-West Trade and Technology Transfer* (Durham, N.C.:, Duke University Press, 1988), pp. 114-115.

35. Jonathan B. Schwartz, "Controlling Nuclear Proliferation: Legal Strategies of the United States," *Law and Policy in International Business*, 20, 1 (1988), p. 25.

36. National Academy of Sciences, *Balancing the National Interest: U.S. National Security Export Controls and Global Economic Competition* (Washington, D.C.: National Academy Press, 1987), p. 113.

37. U.S. General Accounting Office, *Export Controls: Extent of DOD Influence on Licensing Decisions*, (Washington, D.C.: U.S. Government Printing Office, 1989).

38. Smaldone, "U.S. Commercial Arms Exports," p. 194.

39. Ibid.

40. U.S. General Accounting Office, *Report by the General Accounting Office on Arms Export Licensing at the Department of State* (Washington, D.C.: U.S. Government Printing Office, 1987).

41. GAO, *Extent of DOD Influence on Licensing Decisions.*

42. Berman and Garson, "United States Export Controls," pp. 793-794.

43. David W. Danjczek, statement on behalf of the Electronics Industries Association Before the Subcommittee on International Economic Policy and Trade and The Subcommittee on Arms Control, International Security and Science, Committee on Foreign Affairs, U.S. House of Representatives, July 18, 1988, pp. 5-12.

44. Peter F. McCloskey, statement on behalf of the Electronic Industries Association and the Aerospace Industries Association Before the Subcommittee on Arms Control, International Security and Science,

Committee on Foreign Affairs, U.S. House of Representatives, March 9, 1989, p. 3.

45. Senator Heinz's office files.

46. Senator Heinz's office files.

47. *Balancing the National Interest*, pp. 167-177.

48. Ninth Battle Act Report, 1957, in Metzger, *Law of International Trade*, p. 1068.

49. *Inside U.S. Trade*, November 24, 1989.

50. Ibid.

51. U.S. Department of Commerce, *U.S. Trade in Transition: Maintaining the Gains*, a Report to the President from the President's Export Council, Vol. 1, (Washington, D.C.: U.S. Government Printing Office, 1988).

52. U.S. Department of Commerce, *Report of the President's Export Council Subcommittee on Export Administration, 1985-1989*, 2 Vols (Washington, D.C.: U.S. Government Printing Office, 1989).

53. Business Roundtable, *Focus on the Future: A Global Export Control Framework*, Business Roundtable, January, 1990. Cited with permission.

2

The Coordinating Committee for Multilateral Export Controls and the Battle Act

[COCOM] is dogma.
--Italian President Francesco Cossiga, October 13, 1989

The Cold War and Its Impact on Export Controls

World War II transformed the United States into a global power for the first time in its history. At the same time, the United States also faced a major new rival for that status, the Soviet Union. By the end of the war, the Soviet Union occupied most of Central and Eastern Europe. Although the Soviet army posed a threat to Europe, the Soviet Union's weaknesses in naval and air power and nuclear weapons kept it from threatening the national security of the United States. U.S. economic defense policy in the immediate postwar period was therefore based on "selective controls, which deny absolutely the export of war materiel to the Soviet bloc and allow lesser strategic materials to pass only if a net security advantage is gained in return from such trade."[1]

The latter objective was telling. In the aftermath of the war, the United States also had needs. So that it could transform its economy for peacetime, the United States had to export more goods and import strategic raw materials. By 1947 U.S. exports accounted for nearly one-third of total world exports. U.S. foreign trade depended heavily on the export of automobiles, trucks, machine tools, steel, and farm machinery. Wheat accounted for nearly one-half of all agricultural exports.

Finding Markets for U.S. Goods

The question that occupied U.S. officials in the immediate postwar period was to what markets would the United States sell? The U.S. government had one answer. "Immediately after World War II, the United States was hopeful that there would be a revival of the traditional pattern of pre-war East-West trade to aid in the recovery of Europe. Eastern Europe could provide urgently needed fuel, foodstuffs, and timber in exchange for the machinery, equipment, and consumer goods which were in short supply in the East."[2]

Eastern Europe's promise, however, had to be weighed against the growing Soviet sphere of influence. Although the Soviet Union had not yet drawn the iron curtain around Eastern Europe in the first few years after the war, Communist movements in Poland, Romania, Bulgaria, Hungary, and Yugoslavia were becoming entrenched and poised to grab political power. The most tragic case was Czechoslovakia, an independent country whose ties to the West were severed and democratic political process crushed by the Communist movement in February 1948. As one Eastern European country after another was brought into its sphere of influence, the Soviet Union signed bilateral treaties designed to prevent the United States from gaining access to the region.

U.S. foreign aid policy did not help either. As early as 1946, the U.S. foreign aid policy denied Eastern Europe loans or aid, including the denial of a crucial Export-Import Bank loan to Czechoslovakia which eventually helped to topple the pro-Western Czech government. And shades of *perestroika* today: in 1946 the Soviet Union's request for a billion dollar loan to assist in its economic reconstruction program was also denied.

Political events in Europe were far outstripping economic planning. On March 12, 1947, President Truman extended aid to Greece and Turkey in what came to be known as the Truman Doctrine: U.S. policy was to support free peoples who were resisting subjugation and pressures from the outside. The Soviet Union heard the message loud and clear, even though Soviet links to Greece and Turkey were questionable. In July 1947 an anonymous article published in *Foreign Affairs* urged the United States to adopt a "policy of firm containment" of the Soviet Union, which, with the Truman Doctrine, became the basis for U.S. foreign policy in the period of the Cold War.[3] So the question remained: Where were the new markets to come from?

The Marshall Plan

By 1947 nearly $10 billion had been funneled into Europe by the United States, the United Nations Relief and Rehabilitation Administration (UNRRA), the World Bank, and the International Monetary Fund (IMF) without any appreciable improvement in European economies. Indeed, European countries that received foreign aid were plagued by trade deficits, particularly with the United States.

On June 5, 1947, Secretary of State George C. Marshall delivered a 1500-word commencement address at Harvard University that was to change the course of history in Europe. *All* European nations, he suggested, should initiate a collective plan for Europe's economic recovery.

In the summer of 1948, the United States, the United Kingdom, France, *and* the Soviet Union met in Paris to discuss the implementation of the European Recovery Program. With the Truman and containment doctrines still reverberating in the Soviet Union, the Soviets bolted Paris and in the process forced their Eastern European satellites, including a reluctant Czechoslovakia, to reject participation in the plan. The Soviets were not eager to see an Eastern Europe awash in U.S. dollars.

The Congress debated the Economic Cooperation Act (the Marshall Plan) with the coup in Czechoslovakia still fresh and the crisis growing in Germany (the Berlin blockade occurred in June 1948). A sixteen-nation conference in Europe proposed that the recovery program would need $28 billion over a five-year period. The Congress approved $4 billion dollars for the first year, and before the plan ended in 1952 nearly $13 billion had been infused into the economies of the recipient countries. The plan achieved its desired purpose: The European markets began their road to recovery; the U.S. economy prospered accordingly.

Establishing the Machinery of COCOM

The events in Eastern Europe had a direct effect on the establishment of a multilateral export control system. In the atmosphere of the coup in Czechoslovakia and the Berlin blockade, "agreement was shortly reached on a multilateral organization."[4] Secretly tucked into the folds of the Marshall Plan were the origins of a multilateral export control system that in time became known as the Coordinating Committee for Multilateral Export Controls, or COCOM.[5]

On March 26, 1948, the President's Cabinet recommended the initiation of a program to control multilaterally "selective" export controls by Marshall Plan members. In September 1948, the U.S. special representative of the Economic Cooperation Act (ECA) in Europe opened discussions with Marshall Plan recipients regarding "parallel action on the basis of U.S. security control lists."[6]

During 1948-1949, the United States entered into a series of bilateral negotiations with Marshall Plan recipient countries to establish a multilateral strategic export control system to protect Western security. Agreement was reached on imposing an embargo on shipments to the Soviet bloc of arms, ammunition, implements of war, and atomic energy items where this prohibition was not already being applied by individual countries. The negotiations also included controls on "industrial materials and equipment," or what today are known as dual-use items.

In November 1949, the bilateral list negotiations were transferred to a multilateral forum in Paris. The United States, the United Kingdom, France, Italy, the Netherlands, Belgium, and Luxembourg created an informal Consultative Group, composed of senior government officials and the rough equivalent of today's high-level meeting. Membership was shortly expanded to include Norway, Denmark, Canada, and the Federal Republic of Germany. Subsequently, Portugal, Greece, Turkey, and Japan (1954) were added, bringing the total membership to fifteen.[7]

In January 1950 the Consultative Group convened for its initial meeting in Paris and agreed to the following:

1. informal and voluntary organization, with decisions based on consensus;
2. the creation of a Coordinating Committee (COCOM) to oversee the day-to-day tasks of coordinating the multilateral export control system, overseeing enforcement, and recommending improvement measures;
3. COCOM's main function, which would be to oversee trade controls toward the Soviet bloc;
4. the criteria for adding and deleting items from the International List, and the adoption of the "general exceptions" provision for permitting the export of controlled goods on the list on a case-by-case basis;
5. the classification of all COCOM activities as secret to prevent public disclosure of proprietary information useful to the proscribed countries, other free-world countries, and commercial interests among the members.[8]

In 1952 the Consultative Group completed the machinery with the addition of one structural feature, the China Committee (CHINCOM), and one procedural feature, the import certificate-delivery verification (IC/DV) system. In 1954 COCOM undertook its first streamlining attempt at the control lists, an issue still with us today.

The China Committee

The Communist victory in the Chinese civil war was all but a foregone conclusion during COCOM's formative years. In June 1949, when the Chinese Communists announced that China's foreign policy "leaned" to the side of the Soviet bloc, the United States and several European allies placed unilateral trade controls on China. China's entry into the Korean War in December 1950, led the United States to place a trade embargo on both strategic and nonstrategic trade with China. Prior to 1951, U.S. exports to China had been relatively modest--and declining: $354 million in 1947, $273 million in 1948, $83 million in 1949, and $47 million in 1950.[9]

The allies agreed to embargo strategic items, but not nonstrategic ones. Free-world exports to China of nonstrategic items in 1951 totaled $433 million but dropped to $257 million in 1952 as a result of the embargo and China's own policy of self-sufficiency.[10] Imports from China dried up for all intents and purposes by 1952.

The "China Differential." The main responsibility of CHINCOM was to administer the so-called China differential list that contained trade controls toward China, North Korea, and North Vietnam. The China differential was more extensive and stringent than those COCOM administered toward the Soviet bloc. The China control list included about 200 items in addition to those under various levels of control to the Soviet bloc. In 1956 the United Kingdom raised the issue of relaxing the China control list by bringing it on par with COCOM's control list toward the Soviet bloc, but the United States refused. In May 1957 the Consultative Group met in Paris to reconcile the divergent views. When the United States refused once again to relax controls toward China, several group members, including the United Kingdom, unilaterally eliminated the China differential.[11] Subsequently, the China control list was abolished and CHINCOM integrated into COCOM.

U.S. Postscript. The United States maintained the differential until April 14, 1971, when President Richard Nixon announced the end of the twenty-one-year embargo on trade with China. In 1972 the U.S. government relaxed trade restrictions further by making the control level of trade with China comparable to U.S. trade policy toward the Soviet Union. According to the State Department,

At the beginning of 1972, it is clearly in our national interest to pursue prospects for expanded peaceful trade with the P.R.C. and East European Communist countries. The Eastern European market is a dynamic one. The China market may be opening to American goods. . . . A basic premise in exploring these trade possibilities is that we should continue to exercise sufficient governmental control to assure that goods and technology of strategic significance that could be used to the detriment of our national security are not sold to Communist countries.[12]

The Import Certificate-Delivery Verification System

The IC/DV system was a special export control documentation system designed to deter the transshipment or other diversion of controlled goods to the Soviet bloc. Under the IC/DV system, officials from an exporting country could require an import certificate issued to the importer and recorded by the importing government before issuing an export license for a controlled item. The import certificate assures that the shipment in question is actually destined for that country and will not be diverted or reexported, under penalties established by both the importing and exporting governments. The delivery verification certificate confirms that the exported item is actually delivered to the country for which it was originally licensed.

The COCOM Control Lists

In early 1949, the United Kingdom and France formulated an Anglo-French List of strategic items that was similar to, but less comprehensive than, the U.S. Positive List of controlled goods. The UK and France successfully urged Marshall Plan participants to adopt this list as the first multilaterally agreed control list.

The Consultative Group drew up three International Lists: I (embargo of dual-use items), II (quantitative control), and III (exchange of information and surveillance). By April 1952, the three International Lists contained about 400 items, or about 100 fewer than the U.S. Positive List, the forerunner to the Commodity Control List.[13]

The 1954 Streamlining Conference. By the time of Stalin's death in 1953, Soviet economic planning had created serious problems within the Soviet Union and the bloc. The standard of living was steadily declining, and agriculture and industry were competing, unsuccessfully, for scarce resources. In summer 1953 came the "electrifying news of rioting in East Germany."[14] In summer and fall 1953 the entire bloc was engaged in "new economic courses" to solve economic difficulties. One of the components of the "new economic courses" was to expand foreign trade. The Soviet Union, for example, concluded first-ever trade agreements with France and Greece, two members of NATO. This trade offensive was accompanied by a diplomatic offensive, leading the State Department to remark that "the Soviet bloc has shifted some of its priorities."[15]

The Soviet trade offensive triggered the United States' wide-ranging review of its trade policy toward the Soviet bloc, including a thorough reevaluation of U.S. and COCOM export control policies. The State Department described the results:

> By late 1953 the belief was spreading that the strategic trade control program needed reshaping to meet the new problems and outlook. . . . The recognition grew in the United States that the general effort to expand the strategic lists had plainly reached the point of diminishing returns . . . and that a thorough review of them was needed. Officials were convinced that there was need for *more efficient enforcement* [emphasis added] of all regulations, for more supplementary controls to prevent circumvention, and for the upgrading of some items. . . . The United States decided to concentrate its efforts upon preserving and tightening controls on those items of significant evaluation.[16]

The 1954 List Review. In January 1954 the United States and its allies undertook an item-by-item review of their respective control lists. "Being more heavily dependent on foreign trade in general than the United States," the State Department concluded, "the Western European countries were more receptive to the idea of East-West trade than the U.S." [17] The United States and the allies, however, kept their wits about them during the preliminary stages. There was general agreement among the allies that the Soviet Union still intended to drive a wedge among the allies, "feed the economy, especially the industrial-military base," and "weaken multilateral control of trade in strategic materials."[18]

On April 13, the Consultative Group instructed COCOM to undertake a comprehensive review of the control lists. Between July 19 and 21, COCOM completed its review and agreed to:

1. reduce List I from about 260 items to about 170, List II from ninety to about twenty items, and List III from about 100 items to about sixty;
2. leave untouched the munitions and nuclear control lists;
3. strengthen enforcement procedures, including transit and transaction controls following a "tighter but more selective" concept;
4. leave unaltered the China differential.[19]

Despite the revisions, trade between the allies and the Soviet bloc increased in the following two years.[20] From 1954 to 1955 two-way trade between the allies and the Soviet bloc increased by 25 percent to nearly $4.5 billion. In 1956, two-way trade increased once again by 20 percent over 1955.

By 1955 following conclusions of the review, COCOM had developed most, if not all, of the policies, procedures, and problems still extant today.

The Battle Act

By 1950 the Export Control Act restricted U.S. exports of strategic items, and COCOM restricted the export of strategic items multilaterally. The two systems, however, reached but fifteen countries at the time. Nonetheless, some COCOM and several non-COCOM countries continued to trade with the Soviet bloc and had even entered into agreements with the Soviet bloc for trade of nonstrategic items that the U.S. considered "strategic" for reasons of short supply.

In early March 1951, a special subcommittee of the House Foreign Affairs Committee began to hold hearings in executive session on two bills designed to strengthen East-West trade controls and improve their administration. The subcommittee wrote the Battle Bill (H.R. 4550), named for the chairperson of the subcommittee, Representative Laurie C. Battle (D-AL). In August the Senate Foreign Relations Committee approved the bill and on October 26 the President signed it into law. The bill became the Mutual Defense Assistance Control Act of 1951 (P.L. 213), commonly called the Battle Act. The act went into full effect on January 24, 1952.[21]

The legacies of the act are mixed. The Battle Act declared that the United States would embargo the shipment of arms, ammunition, and implements of war, atomic energy materials, petroleum, transportation materials of strategic value, and items of primary strategic significance to the Soviet bloc. It stipulated that no U.S. military, economic, or financial assistance would be provided "to any nation unless it applies an embargo" against the Soviet bloc.[22]

The act also established the legal basis for U.S. participation in COCOM (Sec. 302a, Title III). To administer the program, the act provided for a Battle Act administrator located in the Department of State to "coordinate . . . the various U.S. departments . . . concerned with security controls over exports from other countries."[23] (Harold E. Stassen was the first administrator).

The administrator, in turn, created the machinery for U.S. participation in COCOM. The coordinating staff was--and is--known as the Economic Defense Advisory Committee (EDAC), composed of eleven departments or agencies at the time (State, Defense, Commerce, Treasury, CIA, Office of Defense Mobilization (ODM), Atomic Energy Commission (AEC), Agriculture, the Export-Import (ExIm) Bank, Interior, and the Foreign Operations Administration, which oversaw the act). The EDAC was "purely advisory. . . . It takes no actions, but submits recommendations for actions" regarding U.S. participation in COCOM.[24]

The act also provided for the creation of still another control list. On November 25, 1951, the Battle Act administrator established an embargo list, which went into effect on January 24, 1952. The list was divided into two parts: Category A, which contained twenty-one listings covering items representing arms, ammunition, implements of war, and atomic energy materials; and Category B, which contained ten broad categories covering 264 items commonly known as "dual-use" commodities today: metalworking machinery, chemical and petroleum equipment, electrical and power-generating equipment, general industrial equipment, transportation equipment, electronic and precision instruments, metals, minerals and their manufacture, chemicals, petroleum products, and rubber and rubber products. [25]

In addition, the act stipulated that the United States negotiate with other countries to control *their* strategic items deemed critical *by the United States*. Failure to agree could also jeopardize U.S. financial and economic assistance. Because of their sensitivity, these lists were classified.

The act permitted for Presidential exceptions. From January 24, 1952, through December 31, 1956, the President announced twenty-nine cases, involving seven countries, in which he determined that exceptions should be made to the termination of aid.[26] The act was invoked only once: in 1952 against Ceylon (which was not receiving U.S. aid in any case), for exporting rubber to China in exchange for rice. The sanction continued until 1956 when Malaysia, Singapore, and the UK announced their initial intentions to lift their embargoes of rubber to China. [27]

Two experts consider the Battle Act to have had one "principal positive effect": to provide the legal basis for U.S. participation in COCOM. Otherwise, they call it a "misguided piece of legislation" that if repealed "would sink with hardly a trace."[28] Their principal criticism is that the act "brought pressure on friendly nations not to export to Communist countries items that are not even proscribed by the Battle Act" itself.[29] They also objected to the act's coercive nature, particularly against smaller countries dependent on U.S. aid.[30]

The State Department also noted problems with the Battle Act ten years after it was adopted. The act was losing its effectiveness, State noted, because of the "emergence of a number of new nations and the evolution of a less perfectly monolithic Soviet bloc."[31] The State Department was particularly concerned that the act could be seen by the newly emerging countries as a threat to their "newly achieved freedom": The terms of the Act . . . have the effect of barring the use of Presidential discretion in cases where the United States cannot obtain necessary assurances from an aid-recipient country, but where the use of discretion to permit nonmilitary aid would otherwise be in the national interest. The Battle Act must be more responsive to this type of situation."[32]

The act nonetheless remained in force until it was superseded by the Export Administration Act of 1979.

Notes

1. *A Program for the Denial of Strategic Goods to the Soviet Bloc*, First Battle Act Report, 1952, p. 1. The Battle Act reports are perhaps the most valuable sources of information on the origins and workings of COCOM.

2. Ibid., p. 5.

3. The author of the article signed by they mysterious "Mr. X" was, of course, George F. Kennan, then director of the State Department's Policy Planning Staff. See, "The Sources of Soviet Conduct," *Foreign Affairs* 25 (July 1947).

4. Seventeenth Battle Act Report, 1964, p. 2.

5. All COCOM activities including the location of the organization were classified "secret." It has only been in the past few years that COCOM's location in Paris was revealed.

6. *The Strategic Trade Control System, 1948-1956*, Ninth Report to Congress (1957) on Operations under the Mutual Defense Assistance Control Act of 1951 (the Battle Act Report), in Metzger, *Law of International Trade*, p. 1063. This report is generally considered the best source on the origins of COCOM.

7. Ibid., p. 1064. Beginning on January 1, 1951, Japan's trade was controlled by the Supreme Commander for the Allied Powers (SCAP). SCAP, for example, tightened controls on China after China's entry into the Korean War. Export license applications and approval for exports to China, North Korea, Hong Kong, Macao, and all other destinations required SCAP approval. When the U.S.-Japan peace treaty was signed on April 28, 1952, the Japanese government assumed full control of its export control program and presumably became a full member of COCOM. Spain was admitted to COCOM in 1985 and Australia in 1989, bringing the current total membership to nineteen. Although the initial membership was drawn from NATO countries (except Japan and Iceland, which never joined), COCOM was and is independent of NATO and the Organization for European Economic Cooperation. The U.S. delegation

to COCOM is attached to the U.S. mission to the OECD for administrative purposes only.

8. Ibid., p. 1065.

9. Third Battle Act Report, 1953, p. 34.

10. Ibid., p. 35.

11. Fourteenth Battle Act Report, 1957-1960, p. 5.

12. Twenty-fourth Battle Act Report, 1971, p. 4.

13. Ninth Battle Act Report, 1957, in Metzger, *Law of International Trade*, pp. 1063-1064.

14. "East-West Trade Trends," in Fourth Battle Act Report, 1953, p. 12.

15. Ibid., p. 26.

16. Ninth Battle Act Report, 1957, *Law of International Trade*, in Metzger, pp. 1070-1071.

17. Ibid., p. 1072.

18. Ibid., pp. 1072-1073.

19. Ibid., p. 1076.

20. Ibid., p. 1078.

21. Ninth Battle Act Report, 1957, *Law of International Trade*, in Metzger, p. 1059.

22. First Battle Act Report, 1952, p. 31.

23. Third Battle Act Report, 1953, pp. 44-45.

24. Ibid.

25. Ibid. Appendix B lists Category A items; Appendix C lists Category B items, pp. 37-44.

26. Ninth Battle Act Report, 1957, in Metzger, *Law of International Trade*, p. 1061.

27. Harold J. Berman and John R. Garson, "United States Export Controls--Past, Present, and Future," *Columbia Law Review*, 67, 5 (May 1967), p. 837.

28. Ibid., p. 838.

29. Ibid., pp. 837-838.

30. Ibid.

31. Fifteenth Battle Act Report, 1962, in Metzger, *Law of International Trade*, pp. 1087-1088.

32. Ibid., p. 1088.

3

National Security Interests

The "Proscribed Destinations"

The Export Administration Act of 1979, as amended, states that it is the policy of the United States

> to encourage trade with all countries with which we have diplomatic or trading relations, except those countries with which such trade has been determined by the President to be against the national interest . . . [and] to restrict the export of goods and technology which would make a signficant contribution to the miiltary potential of any other country or combination of countries which would prove detrimental to the national security of the United States.

For reasons of security, the United States--and COCOM--control the export of militarily significant goods and commodities to the following countries: the Soviet Union, Albania, Bulgaria, Czechoslovakia, Hungary, Mongolian People's Republic, Poland, Romania, North Korea, Vietnam, and the People's Republic of China. The United States, but not COCOM, applies unilateral controls for national security reasons to Cambodia, Cuba, and Laos. This chapter will analyze U.S. export control policy toward the Soviet Union, the Warsaw Pact, and China. There are no changes in controls contemplated or recommended for the remaining countries.

The Soviet Union

The Soviet Union is not my enemy.[1]
                                --William J. Crowe, Chairman, U.S. Joint Chiefs of Staff

Any discussion of the threat to the national security interests of the United States and its allies must begin with an assessment of the threat posed by the Soviet Union and its allies. Such an evaluation, in turn, must take into account Soviet rhetoric as well as actions.

Theory

Since 1985, three concepts introduced by Soviet Party Secretary-General and President Mikhail Gorbachev have formed the foundation for the current reform movement under way in the Soviet Union and Eastern Europe: *perestroika*, the theoretical underpinning for the economic "restructuring" program: *glasnost* or "openness," the tolerance of open debate and more objective reporting on political and social affairs; and *democrazatsiya* or "democratization," the provision of some electoral choice in political affairs. In addition, the military has also adopted a new doctrine called "reasonable sufficiency" or "defensive sufficiency," depending on whether one sees the proverbial glass half full or half empty. In all these areas, it is my view that, on balance, practice is outstripping theory, a not uncommon occurrence in societies undergoing convulsive changes.

Perestroika.   *Perestroika* is the best known, and perhaps least understood, of Gorbachev's key concepts. *Perestroika's* rhetoric, Gorbachev says, is not hostile because "hostile rhetoric also ruins relations."[2] But *perestroika*, he makes clear, is about reforming Marxian economics and Leninist politics, not discarding them: "The policy of restructuring puts everything in its place. We are fully restoring the principle of socialism: 'From each according to his ability, to each according to his work.'"[3] Or, as Gorbachev explains,

> The end result of perestroika is clear.... it is a thorough renewal of every aspect of Soviet life; it is giving socialism the most progressive forms of social organization . . . the essence of perestroika lies in the fact that *it unites socialism with democracy* [his emphasis] and *revives the Leninist concept* [my emphasis] of socialist construction both in theory and in practice.[4]

Gorbachev describes *perestroika* as a "revolution" in the socioeconomic and cultural development of Soviet society. However, to the extent that *perestroika* seeks to preserve the present form of government, it is not revolutionary. This distinction is crucial. To be sure, political revolutions are occurring in Central and Eastern Europe, where one form of government--communist--is being replaced by another--democratic. These political revolutions will be discussed in the next section.

Glasnost *and* Democrazatsiya. *Glasnost* and *democrazatsiya*, the other major concepts in Gorbachev's new program, also have their limitations. The concepts are used interchangeably with "democracy," "human rights," and "freedom" but have little resemblance to these values as they are practiced in the West. This is a crucial distinction. At the end of the day, the Soviet Union's political value system will in all probability be fundamentally different from, and in opposition to the political value system of the West.

The introduction of such liberal measures as semifree elections and local autonomy is touted as evidence that the Soviet political system has adopted a process whereby the people's political will and thought of self-determination will be made manifest. Gorbachev, however, again goes to great lengths to make clear that self-determination, like *perestroika*, has limitations: It may be fine for local elections, sharing local political power with the party, or economic reform programs modeled after those in the West or even China, but it is not intended to curtail the monopoly of Communist political power in those institutions that interact with foreigners. Not surprisingly, in the early stages of political change in the bloc, Communists have remained or are struggling to remain in key positions in the foreign and defense ministries of the Eastern European countries undergoing change.

As a foreign policy concept, *glasnost*'s meaning is evolving, seemingly beyond Gorbachev's initial intention and almost certainly beyond his control. Gorbachev claims that the framework of political relations between socialist countries "must be strictly based on absolute independence." And events are forcing his hand. Although he does not say it in his book *Perestroika*, his view that Third World nations have the right to be their own bosses appears to be taking hold in Central and Eastern Europe and the Baltics, but again within limitations for the present.

At the very least, Soviet doctrine on political change in the bloc has become more colorful. Leonid Brezhnev's dour and heavy-handed policy as exemplified by the Czech intervention has been replaced by the jaunty slogans of spokesman Gennadi Gerasimov, who dubbed Gorbachev's laissez-faire approach to Eastern Europe the "Sinatra doctrine--I did it my way."[5]

During the Chautauqua Conference on U.S.-Soviet Relations held at the University of Pittsburgh on November 2, 1989, Nikolai V. Shishlin, senior staff member of the Central Committee of the Soviet Communist party, was asked why the Soviet Union, if it was so concerned about ending regional conflicts, did not end its "occupation" of Lithuania, Estonia, and Latvia. Shishlin said the Soviet Union was trying to amend its constitution so that it would have a federated republic, "not just on paper, but in reality." He added: "We want to create a true republic where each republic could determine its own fate. Therefore, there can be no talk at all of any use of force in the Baltic. I think we'll be able to resolve the problems in a reasonable, democratic manner."[6]

This position has the Soviets in the horns of a dilemma. On November 27, the Soviet legislature voted to grant the three Baltic republics economic autonomy beginning January 1, 1990. This move ostensibly gives the region full control over its land and resources--but not its political machinery. On December 20, Lithuania's Communist party broke with Moscow, "becoming the first in the history of the Soviet Union to declare itself independent of the national party."[7] Three days later, Gorbachev, "in one of his most emotional speeches since taking office," accused supporters of the nationalist independence groups in the Baltic region of trying to "blow up" the country and sow "discord, bloodshed and death."[8] He made it clear that he "would not tolerate movements in the Baltics, the Caucasus and elsewhere that support secession from the Soviet Union."[9]

In the larger realm of security, *glasnost* does not deal with the heady problem of an Eastern Europe without the Warsaw Pact; indeed, the Warsaw Pact's decision to extend its charter tells us to expect military alliances in Europe in the next decade, albeit in a different form.

"Reasonable Sufficiency": The New Military Doctrine. Soviet military power in Eastern Europe has historically served as a security blanket in two fundamental ways: as a buffer against NATO and as the guarantor of political legitimacy for some of the state structures established after World War II. The first mission of Soviet military power remains unchanged, although in the transition period its internal structure appears to be undergoing reform.

It is in the second mission that the most profound change appears to be taking place. For example, students of Soviet politics believe that Gorbachev played an important *indirect* role in the ouster of East Germany's party leader Erich Honecker by signaling that 380,000 Soviet troops in East Germany would not be used to put down the demonstrations for greater freedoms.[10] Bulgaria's Todor Zhivkov was given the same message. [11]

Returning to the first mission, what does Gorbachev *say* about Soviet military power? Why, he asks, does the Soviet Union maintain and modernize its weapons and armed forces? Because, he answers, the Soviet Union "has been under permanent threat of potential aggression." Still, he argues, the Soviet Union is prepared to disarm. But is it? "Reasonable sufficiency," the new Soviet military doctrine, includes strategic and conventional force reductions. The concept is, he argues, a defensive program. But as the U.S. Joint Chiefs of Staff make clear, the current Soviet security concept projects a military force structure of 4.6 million men under arms in the next decade.

Current proposals to reduce substantially the force structures of NATO and the Warsaw Pact will not be completed, if agreed to, until the late 1990s. The Intermediate-Range Nuclear Forces (INF) agreement will not be fully implemented until the early 1990s. A Strategic Arms Reduction Talks (START) agreement would also not bring about a decrease in strategic forces in the immediate future. So there will be a period during which military practice will lag behind the political program, and pacing the Western response to change in this period becomes the chief challenge to U.S. and allied governments, particularly in the area of liberalizing export controls to the Soviet Union.

Perestroika *and Technology*. Finally, what does Gorbachev say in his book about the role of technology? In his sweeping analysis of Soviet economic problems, he blames Soviet technological backwardness on Soviet "naivete," singling out the Western high technology embargo as a contributing factor.

Gorbachev's admission is, perhaps, an indication that the multilateral export control system may have worked, were it not for Soviet successes in technology theft. The lesson learned, he writes, was to direct Soviet development policies inwardly, within the bloc, to put an end to the "import scourge" and to spur indigenous advances in Soviet science and technology. He reveals that the June 1986 meeting of the Communist party's Central Committee established a program for the modernization of science and technology with an emphasis on developing machine-tool building, instrument making, electronics, and electrical engineering. As a result, "the Soviets in fact have the largest research and development base in the world."[12]

According to John Kiser, president of a technology-transfer and venture company specializing in the Soviet bloc, under *perestroika*, "the West may be able to acquire much more technology from the Soviet defense sector than has been available in the past."[13] Kiser assails the U.S. government's reluctance to encourage high technology trade with the Soviet Union in such "exotic areas of space power, explosion welding, high frequency radio wave generators, pulsed power devices and advanced ceramics manufacture."[14]   Likening the U.S. government's attitude to "lean[ing] against the candy store window and dream[ing] of getting its hands on the goodies," he then suggests that trade with the Soviet Union "will help us by altering our mindset about our relationship with other cultures."[15]

There are three problems with Kiser's proposals. First, the technologies he suggests for bilateral trade are precisely the technologies with the most significant capability for military end-uses. The U.S. government should not be in the business of improving Soviet military capabilities, at least not for the near future. Second, there are questions about the quality of some Soviet technologies. Consider the following three examples, concerning machine tools, computers, and fiber optics.

Machine tools, which received considerable public attention as a result of the diversion of several propeller milling machines by a Japanese firm to the Soviet Union in the mid-1980s, flourished before *perestroika* was announced but became the first high technology in the Soviet Union to obtain direct foreign-trade rights under Gorbachev in   1987.[16] Soviet-manufactured machine tools are currently exported to Japan, West Germany, Switzerland, and the Netherlands, among other   countries;[17] yet there is considerable disagreement among the U.S. government, its COCOM partners, and trade consultants like Kiser over whether the tools meet Western standards. Currently, COCOM's policy is to restrict export to the Soviet Union of machines with more than two simultaneously controlled axes of motion. In the Toshiba diversion case discussed in Chapter 4, four of the Toshiba propeller milling machines had nine axes and another four had five axes.

Computers are integral to *perestroika*'s success.[18]   According to the National Research Council, in the planned distribution of computer investment for the entire Soviet economy at the end of 1985, industry accounted for 64 percent, transportation and communications 9.1 percent, and agriculture 2.8 percent. Between 1986 and 1990, investment in the computer industry was to rise from 100 to 140 percent.[19]   Although the evidence suggests that the Soviets have not met their targets and development of the computer industry is still relatively slow, computers nonetheless play a key role in Soviet economic reforms and bear watching, as the case study on the liberalization of personal computers by the U.S. government will show.

During the period of détente (1972-77), the Soviet Union *legally* purchased about $245 million in goods from the West, of which $120 million were U.S. computers.[20]   In the meantime, the Soviet Union receives most of its computers, mainly VAX clones,[21] from manufacturers in Hungary, Bulgaria, Czechoslovakia, Yugoslavia, and what was formally East Germany.[22]   These countries have also made a big business out of cloning IBM mainframes.[23]   As for Soviet computer manufacturing capabilities, the Soviet computing industry has "failed to provide a microelectronics base sufficient to match Western developments and provide for mass production of everything from personal computers to large mainframes."[24] To the best of our knowledge, the Soviet Union does not have a supercomputer.

There is no lack of interest among Western computer firms in assisting the Soviet Union in acquiring the capability of manufacturing computers that meet Western standards. The National Research Council notes the "proliferation of proposed joint ventures relating to computer products and computer controls" between Western and Soviet firms. One joint venture would allow the Soviets to make Soviet designed IBM-XT clones using Asian parts and software for sale in the Soviet Union. Other joint ventures would assist the Soviets in developing software using MS/DOS and LOTUS 1-2-3.[25] For the moment, existing export controls have blocked such efforts, but, as shall be seen in the discussion on joint ventures, the problem is just beginning.

The modernization of the Soviet Union's telecommunications network is among *perestroika*'s highest priorities. This is the area in which the U.S. government and several COCOM members have had the most difficulty in controlling the export of technology to the Soviet Union.

The combined effects of *perestroika* and Eastern Europe's dramatic opening to the West have also bolstered the technology transfer climate regarding fiber optics. A U.S. firm, for example, is heading a consortium to build a $500 million, 19,200 kilometers (12,000-mile) optical fiber communications cable that would span the Soviet Union, linking it to Europe and Japan. Because fiber optics have numerous military applications, including undersea detection of submarines and control of missiles in flight, the export would require approval by COCOM.[26]

This brings us back to the third problem with Kiser's proposals: The Soviet thirst for Western technology remains unquenchable. In the 1970s and 1980s, Moscow launched a massive global program to acquire illegally Western high technologies for Soviet military programs.

Practice

There is some congruence between Gorbachev's words and deeds, but, as Secretary Baker put it before the Foreign Policy Association in New York City on October 16, 1989 "we must not succumb to a false optimism that *perestroika* in Soviet foreign policy has gone far enough and that we can rely on the new thinking to take account of our interests." Yet Gorbachev has built an impressive record since he assumed power in 1985. He followed the introduction of *perestroika* with a series of policies that have had a profound impact on East-West relations. He established *perestroika*'s credibility by such unilateral actions as withdrawing Soviet forces from Afghanistan (although maintaining unacceptable levels of military assistance), presumably pressuring the Cubans to withdraw from Angola (but not pressuring the Cubans to stop arms shipments to Nicaragua and Panama, ensuring regional instability in the Western hemisphere), and announcing unilateral reductions in Warsaw Pact nuclear and conventional forces in Europe. This last action merits a closer look.

Unilateral Troop Reductions. Addressing the United Nations on December 7, 1988, Gorbachev announced that the Soviet army would be reduced significantly before 1990. According to the 1989 edition of the Department of Defense's annual assessment of the Soviet army, *Soviet Military Power*, the unilateral cuts were to include 500,000 troops (50,000 from Eastern Europe), six combat divisions (all from Eastern Europe), 10,000 tanks (5,300 from Eastern Europe), 800 aircraft (all from Eastern Europe), 8,500 artillery systems (all from Eastern Europe), and short-range nuclear systems associated with the six tank divisions.

In summary, the Warsaw Pact countries have pledged to reduce their combined forces by 581,300 personnel, 12,751 tanks, and 1,010 aircraft. The balance of forces in Europe, however, will remain asymmetrical: nearly three to one in the Warsaw Pact's favor in numbers of tanks and divisions, for example. Nonetheless, Gorbachev is following through with his commitment. According to Congressional sources, at the current pace of reductions, he should achieve his objective on schedule in 1990. Defense analysts, who appear to agree on the substance and reality of the cuts, estimate variously that they will reduce the threat in Eastern Europe from between 5 and 20 percent.

Reduction of the Defense Budget. Gorbachev is also making a convincing argument in his goal to reduce defense spending by 14.2 percent, which would represent, by Soviet estimates, 9 percent of Soviet GNP. According to a new estimate by the CIA, Soviet military spending declined in 1989 by 1.5 percent. The intelligence community now believes that the cuts will be even deeper in 1990, reaching 7 percent.

Gorbachev followed his unilateral policies with a series of successful multilateral initiatives such as round-robin summitry with the United States, China, and Japan and signing the INF Treaty with the United States. Successful START talks would further add to his already impressive record.

Gorbachev's Impact on the West. A popular assumption about a future world war is that Europe will once again be the principal battleground. Gorbachev, who argues that Soviets are Europeans, too, has advanced this notion within the context of a "common European home," which "suggests above all a degree of integration, even if states belong to different social systems and opposing military alliances."[27] He has effectively used the American credo that a nuclear war "cannot be won and must never be fought."

How effective has his message been? As a public relations ploy, very effective. He is perhaps the most popular political leader in Western Europe; in West Germany, for example, he had the approval of more than 90 percent of the public. Nor is the United States immune to his popularity. One recent poll showed that 79 percent of Americans believed Gorbachev to be a fundamentally different kind of Soviet leader, whereas a second poll showed that he enjoyed a 71 percent approval rating compared to President Bush's 76 percent. A November 1989 *Washington Post*-ABC News poll showed that 60 percent of those interviewed had a favorable view of Gorbachev compared to President Bush's 71 percent.[28]

This same poll showed that 46 percent of those interviewed believed the Soviet Union was a "force for peace" compared to 6 percent who believed it in 1983. Forty-five percent believed that Gorbachev "seriously" wanted to make Soviet society more open and democratic compared to 42 percent who believed he was simply creating a good public image to gain an advantage for the Soviet Union. Even so, 52 percent believed that there was a great deal or a good amount of danger that the Soviet Union would revert to its hard-line Communist practice in the future. Finally, *Time* magazine (January 1, 1990) rewarded Gorbachev's five dramatic years as Soviet leader by naming him "Man of the Decade," the first time the magazine has awarded such a distinction. This was followed by the awarding of the 1990 Nobel Peace Prize to Gorbachev.

As a political gambit, Gorbachev's impact has also been very effective. *Perestroika* presents COCOM (and NATO) with its most serious challenge to date. The United Kingdom, Italy, Germany, and France are increasingly questioning the continuation of COCOM's restrictive strategic trade policies toward the Soviet bloc. The United States, the architect of most of these restrictive policies, is finding itself on the defensive and in danger of becoming isolated in COCOM.

Issues in U.S.-Soviet Trade and
Technology Transfer Relations

Both the United States and the Soviet Union have erected serious obstacles to the renewal of trade relations in general, and toward restoring the level of the technology transfer program in place before the Soviet invasion of Afghanistan. For its part, the United States has

TABLE 3.1
U.S.-Soviet Trade, 1980-1988 (in millions of U.S. dollars)

	1980	1981	1982	1983	1984	1985	1986	1987	1988[a]
U.S. exports (FAS)									
Total	1,510	2,339	2,586	2,002	3,282	2,421	1,248	1,480	2,281
Agric	1,047	1,665	1,855	1,457	2,817	1,864	648	923	1,765
Non-Ag	463	677	734	545	466	558	600	557	516
U.S. imports (CIF)									
Total	463	387	248	367	602	441	601	470	415
Agric	10	12	11	11	11	9	16	22	---
Non-Ag	452	375	237	356	591	432	585	448	---
Gold B.	88	22	4	2	2	1	154		---
Trade turnover	1,973	2,726	2,837	2,369	3,885	2,863	1,849	1,950	2,696
U.S. trade balance	+1,047	+1,952	+2,341	+1,635	+2,681	+1,980	+647	+1,010	+2,281

[a] through October 1988
Sources: U.S. Census Bureau, U.S. Department of Commerce, and John Hardt, *U.S.-Soviet Commercial Relations in a Period of Negotiation*. Congressional Research Service. Library of Congress, updated January 19, 1989, p. 3

resolved one issue (rescission of the "no exceptions" policy) and partially resolved another (seeking a waiver of the Jackson-Vanik Amendment of 1974 linking trade to Soviet emigration policy) but has made no progress on a third (establishing a policy toward joint ventures).

Gorbachev controls the outcomes of two areas linked to trade and technology transfer--human rights and technology theft. He appears to be making progress in the first area but not in the second, which is a legitimate barrier to renewing Western exports of advanced technology.

Gorbachev believes that the United States and the Soviet Union do not need each other's trade. He supports the resumption of trade, he says, because it provides a basis for political *rapprochement*. The data (given in Table 3.1) support his view that the two countries have managed to do without each other's trade in the past ten years.

Westerners can be equally cynical. One international trade consultant put it this way:

> In the pre-perestroika Soviet Union, trade with the United States occurred essentially when the Soviets wanted: from 1920 to 1922, when Lenin encouraged foreign investment to develop the Soviet economy; between 1934 and 1938, when the Soviets turned from their traditional partner, Germany; from 1942 to 1945, during the period of lend-lease to aid the war effort, and just after World

War II, when American relief payments were used for reconstruction; in 1964, following a disastrous harvest when Canada was unable to provide the needed supplies of grain; in 1972-73 when trade blossomed in the days of détente and the "great grain robbery"; and in 1979, following an especially poor Soviet harvest, when U.S.-Soviet trade reached a record level.[29]

In 1979 during the latter years of détente and before the Soviet invasion of Afghanistan, bilateral trade reached an all-time high of $4.5 billion. High technology exports accounted for about $50 million. Since 1980, U.S.-Soviet bilateral trade--mainly U.S. exports of agricultural commodities and Soviet exports of energy, raw materials, and gold--has averaged $2.57 billion, with a high of $3.9 billion in 1984 and a low of $1.85 billion in 1986.

Between 1980 and 1988, nearly 74 percent ($1.56 billion) of all U.S. exports to the Soviet Union were agricultural products. According to Gorbachev, the reason the Soviet Union imports U.S. grain is to keep what little trade there is alive. "Otherwise," he says, "it may die."[30] In 1988 bilateral merchandise trade was stillborn: Soviet exports to the United States accounted for only 0.1 percent of total U.S. manufactures imports, and U.S. exports accounted for only 0.2 percent of total Soviet manufactures imports. Commerce Secretary Mosbacher, appearing on national television, said "unfortunately" for U.S.-Soviet trade, the Soviets "don't have much to sell to the United States beyond oil, vodka and caviar."[31] U.S. technology exports, on the other hand, primarily low-end technologies, have averaged $58.3 million since 1980.

Afghanistan and the No Exceptions Policy.[32] On May 29, 1989, President Bush announced the rescission of the "no exceptions" policy instituted after the Soviet invasion of Afghanistan. The policy was to COCOM what short-range nuclear missiles have become for the European members of NATO.

The Soviets invaded Afghanistan on December 26, 1979. On January 4, 1980 the United States reached a decision to freeze high tech exports to the Soviet Union. On January 11, the Carter Administration temporarily implemented the freeze when it suspended nearly 1,000 license applications. The policy was made permanent on March 18, 1980, after an extensive interagency review. This action affected over $300 million in licenses under review.

The United States routinely denied all domestic applications for exports to the Soviet Union of controlled technologies that required a U.S. validated license and referral to COCOM for review. On March 18 the United States denied eight pending cases frozen on January 4 that reveal the extent of U.S. high technology pre-invasion exports. Included on the denial list were such strategic technologies as ballistic protectors and high-strength military structures, digital computing systems and peripheral enhancements for Soviet computers, seismic data-processing equipment, research equipment used in the development of microwave semiconductors, and technical data and equipment for a telecommunications plant. On June 3 the United States extended the policy to cover exports to Afghanistan.

The policy did not apply to agricultural commodities (these goods were covered by the grain embargo), other items deemed essential to public health and safety (a high-level computer for Moscow's airport, for example, was approved for public safety reasons, as were other controlled items for the earthquake in Armenia and the Chernobyl nuclear disaster), or if the export served U.S. and Western national security interests (the communications hot line linking Moscow and Washington, D.C.).

The policy's effectiveness depended on COCOM's compliance and enforcement. COCOM would only agree to review carefully exceptions requests submitted to it; COCOM did not agree to the total embargo. The United States, by dint of its veto power (recall that COCOM operates by consensus), forced COCOM to abandon the policy of case-by-case review, adopted in 1949, of high technology exports to the Soviet Union and Eastern Europe.

The "no exceptions" policy illustrates U.S. use of export controls as an instrument of foreign policy. The policy may have been successful, as Gorbachev admits: It succeeded in keeping highly coveted Western technology from reaching the Soviet bloc by *legal* means. It also failed, however, because the Soviets adopted a highly successful *illegal* program to acquire Western technology through diversion or espionage. In fall 1988, in anticipation of the mid-February 1989 deadline for Soviet withdrawal from Afghanistan, some Western European members of COCOM, led by the United Kingdom, notified the U.S. administration that they would no longer be bound by the "no exceptions" policy. These COCOM countries were responding to nearly ten years of frustration with the policy. The rescission of the "no exceptions" policy is largely symbolic. Cases will now once again be submitted to COCOM. However, the United States still retains its veto over the cases, presuming COCOM members submit them for review. The trend in the past year suggests this has not been happening: Suspicious of the U.S. veto, COCOM members have begun to circumvent COCOM review procedures by refusing to submit cases. The new contentious issue replacing the "no exceptions" policy is the lack of a U.S. policy on joint ventures.

Joint Ventures.   At the December 1987 Washington summit, Secretary-General Gorbachev and President Reagan agreed that "commercially viable joint ventures . . . could play a role in the further development of commercial relations" between the Soviet Union and the United States. In January 1988 the Soviet Union approved a joint venture law to attract Western investments and technology. This was followed by a new foreign trade and investment law in December 1988, easing restrictions on foreign ownership of joint ventures. For example, the law removed the requirement that at least 51 percent of a company be domestically owned and placed a larger emphasis on negotiations to determine the percentages for ownership. These moves have apparently begun to pay off.

According to PlanEcon, a Washington-based consulting firm that promotes trade with the Soviet Union and Eastern Europe, as of October 1, 1989, Soviet joint ventures have reached 940, up nearly fivefold from the 191 registered with PlanEcon on December 31, 1988. Western European and Japanese companies accounted for 595 of the joint ventures, whereas the United States accounted for only 97. Of the approximately 500 clients that receive PlanEcon's data on Eastern Europe, European and Japanese firms account for 75 percent.[33] PlanEcon cites these figures to demonstrate the lack of U.S. interest in joint ventures in the Soviet Union and Eastern Europe. The problem, I submit, is more fundamental: U.S. export controls laws.

Joint ventures rose to the top of the Reagan Administration's export control agenda in summer 1988 with approval of licenses for Honeywell and its U.S. partner, Bailey Controls of Louisiana, to set up joint ventures to supply automated production controls for Soviet fertilizer plants. The cases immediately ran into trouble.

Opponents in and outside the U.S. government argued that joint ventures are one of the main ploys by the Soviet Union to attract Western technology.[34] Because of objections by the Department of Defense and the intelligence community, the cases were escalated to the Export Administration Review Board (EARB), a cabinet-level body chaired by Commerce.

The cases raised two issues, which the administration did not resolve. At the economic policy level, the administration did not address the question of whether the U.S. government was prepared to help the Soviet Union improve its industrial base, and hence its own economic security. Indeed, the administration has yet to confront the issue.

At the technology transfer policy level, the cases raised what may well be the key to the success or failure of joint ventures: how to control the transfer of technical data for process-manufacturing know-how. In the two cases before the EARB, the equipment involved--low end controllers-- was decontrolled and nonstrategic. However, controlled parts and components were embedded in the computer system, making the technical data subject to controls and creating the need for validated licenses, although the technology involved was well below the general exceptions level (formerly, the level of the "no exceptions" policy). Opponents of the joint ventures argued that transferring low-end process technology would open the floodgates for requests for high-end process technology. One opponent said that the "venture would entail the transfer of the necessary machinery and continuing technical support needed to permit the Soviets domestically to produce highly advanced automated control devices. . . . These controls are well suited to the sort of precision manufacturing entailed in the production of modern chemical weapons."[35] The licenses were ultimately issued with specific end-use safeguards, but the marker for protracted interagency disputes in the absence of a policy was laid.

The issue of joint ventures in U.S.-COCOM relations was elevated to the top of COCOM's agenda by the refusal of three COCOM members--the UK, France, and Italy--to submit their cases to COCOM for review because each joint venture contained technologies the United States was prepared to veto. The three argued that the levels of technologies involved were below the "no exceptions" level, a judgment permitted under a COCOM procedure called "national discretion treatment." National discretion permits members to license exports the members have agreed qualify as "administrative exceptions notes," or low-end technologies without referral to COCOM. The assumption is that members have checked the proposed level of the export with the controlled lists and have made a determination that the export is at the low end of the controlled lists and eligible for national discretion treatment. The creation of this procedure was intended to relieve COCOM from reviewing thousands of cases involving low-end technologies. Following is a summary of three of those cases, involving Alcatel telecommunications, Simon-Carves, and Olivetti.[36]

In the early 1980s, Alcatel, N.V., a French computer and telecommunications firm, signed a contract with a Soviet enterprise, Krashna Zarayato, to provide the Soviet Union with telephone digital switching equipment and manufacturing technology. This technology cost ITT, one of Alcatel's parent companies, more than $1 billion to develop. Under the agreement, the Soviet Union was to procure outright the equipment and construct an assembly facility near Leningrad.

In 1984 the United States agreed in COCOM to decontrol the equipment by 1988, by which time it was assumed the Soviet Union would have developed an indigenous capability comparable to the equipment under consideration. By 1988, believing that the Soviet Union had failed to develop a comparable system, the United States raised an objection in COCOM but failed to prevail. Alcatel has made some exports in the past year. This case, the first assault on the no exceptions policy, was a harbinger of things to come.

In 1988 Simon-Carves, a British engineering firm, signed a $450 million contract to build a plant to manufacture factory-automation equipment in Yerevan, the capital of Armenia. The factory, scheduled to be completed in 1991, is to make industrial microcomputers capable of directing precision assembly-line production of printed circuit boards. The United States argues that the level of technology was covered by the control lists and required submission to COCOM. The UK, fearing a veto on equipment it has approved under national discretion treatment, refused to submit the case and has allowed the first shipments to be exported.

The case of Olivetti is similar to that of Simon-Carves in the equipment involved. The United States, however, was successful in persuading the Italian government to downgrade the technology, although the Italian government has also refused to submit the cases to COCOM. (This case should not be confused with another Olivetti case concerning the alleged export of machine tools to the Soviet Union).

Human Rights. Imports and credits are controlled by several domestic laws linking trade to human rights. The most important legal barrier to U.S.-Soviet trade is the Jackson-Vanik amendment to the Trade Act of 1974, which stipulates that most-favored-nation (MFN) tariff treatment may not be granted to any country that restricts emigration. There are, however, several positive developments that augur well for improving this aspect of the economic relationship.

First, in 1988 Soviet emigration to the United States reached record levels. Liberalized Soviet emigration procedures produced a flood of Soviet applications for refugee status that have exceeded Congressional appropriations, annual admissions ceilings determined by the President, and government and private-sector capacity for processing refugees.

As a result, the Department of State reports backlogs in the system. According to U.S. government figures, about 55,000 Soviet citizens sought admission for permanent settlement in FY-89. Most applicants are Soviet Jews, Armenians, and those from other minority groups. Soviet admissions will account for over 25 percent of the total number of refugees admitted to the United States in 1989.

Second, the Bush Administration has labeled U.S. foreign policy and human rights policy toward the Soviet Union a "major success." In his Texas A&M University speech on May 12, 1989, the President gave conditional support for a temporary waiver of Jackson-Vanik restrictions providing the Soviet Union codifies its emigration laws in accordance with international standards. The President's announcement was generally welcomed by influential Jewish groups such as the American Jewish Congress, B'nai B'rith, and the National Conference on Soviet Jewry. In addition, one of the cosponsors of the Jackson-Vanik amendment, former representative Charles Vanik (D-OH), has recommended that Moscow be granted MFN status for an eighteen-month period in recognition of its improved human rights record.

Third, the Reagan Administration gave its conditional support to Moscow's proposal to host a human rights conference in 1991. Fourth, the President's announcement has also led to a reconsideration of the 1974 Stevenson amendment, which places a limit on Ex-Im Bank credits to the Soviet Union without Congressional approval, although no action has occurred yet.

Finally, the United States and the Soviet Union announced November 3, 1989 that for the first time both countries would cosponsor a United Nations General Assembly resolution asking all nations to strengthen the United Nations and defend peace and human rights. According to the announcement, the agreement to cosponsor the resolution "marks the end of Cold War rhetoric at the United Nations and the beginning of a new U.N. Era."[37]

Technology Theft. Moscow's massive, global program to acquire Western technology illegally remains a barrier to improved trade relations with the United States and the West. Indeed, the Soviet Union has engaged in theft and smuggling of embargoed items since the establishment of COCOM. In 1953 the State Department wrote that one of the Soviet Union's "immediate and specific goals" was to "obtain through illicit channels those strategic materials whose shipment [was] restricted by free-world governments in the interest of their national security."[38] Only in the past ten to fifteen years, however, has the Soviet Union raised technology theft to an art form. In the decade coinciding with the technology embargo, Moscow has obtained a significant amount of U.S. and Western technology legally, illegally through diversions, and, as the Walker case revealed, through espionage.

The West has learned much about Soviet priorities for technology acquisition. According to an unclassified CIA assessment based on Soviet documents made available to the West in 1982, the Soviet technology acquisition program has two separate but overlapping parts: an espionage program and an illegal trade program. The espionage program is managed by the Soviet Military Industrial Commission (VPK) and carried out primarily through the Soviet and Eastern European intelligence services. The illegal trade program is managed by the Ministry of Foreign Trade and carried out primarily by Western traders under contract to the Soviets.

According to the CIA, about 60 percent of Moscow's illegally acquired technology in the late 1970s and early 1980s was of U.S. origin, and about 70 percent of the total acquired from all sources is on the COCOM control lists. Table 3.2 is an illustrative but hardly exhaustive list of high technology equipment and technical data obtained illegally by the Soviet Union.

In the late 1970s and into the 1980s, an average of 5,000 Soviet military equipment and weapons systems programs benefited from the 6,000 to 10,000 pieces of hardware and 100,000 documents acquired *annually* through illegal means. The Soviets budgeted roughly $1.4 billion (in 1980 dollars) for the programs, a sum one would think Gorbachev could redirect into economic modernization programs. The problem is that the Soviet Union has become so dependent on Western technology that it is cheaper to steal Western technology than to invest in a sagging R & D sector.

U.S. Export Control Policy Toward the Soviet Union in the Next Decade

President Bush opened the early December 1989 Malta summit by presenting a list of ideas for improving U.S.-Soviet relations. The President targeted the 1990 summit for completing a trade agreement that granted MFN status to the Soviet Union; supporting the Soviet Union's request for observer status in the Uruguay Round of General Agreement on Tariffs and Trade (GATT) talks; expanding U.S.-Soviet technical economic cooperation; lifting statutory restrictions on export credits; beginning discussions on a bilateral investment treaty (BIT); and improving ties between the Soviets and the OECD, human rights, regional issues (particularly Soviet policy in Central America), arms control, military openness, the Olympics, the environment, and student exchanges. Not one word was devoted to export controls and technology transfer.[39]

After a careful analysis of the Soviet threat, I would propose the following conclusions and policy recommendations for export controls and technology transfer:

Continue to Maintain Present Levels of Export Controls Toward the Soviet Union. The Department of Defense's conclusion that "today the likelihood of conflict between the United States and the Soviet Union is perhaps as low as it has been at any time in the post-war era" is on the whole accurate.[40] Nevertheless, the Soviet Union, without regard to the Warsaw Pact (where changes are occurring at breakneck speed), still poses a formidable threat to the West, particularly in light of its massive strategic nuclear capabilities, the superiority in numbers of its vast conventional force, and unabated technology theft programs. Furthermore, Soviet support of regional conflicts remains a serious problem.

TABLE 3.2

Selected Worldwide Soviet Acquisitions and Military Applications of Western Documents, Military Hardware, and Dual-Use Products

Western Technology Acquired	Application/Improvement
Strategic Missiles	
Documents on cruise missiles using radar terrain map	Cruise missile guidance
Documents on heat-shielding material for reentry vehicles	Ballistic missile warheads
Documents on ballistic missile defense concepts	Future ballistic missile defense
Air Defense	
F-14, F-15, F-18, documents on fire controls radar	Four Soviet fighters
US Phoenix missile documents	Air-to-air missiles
Infrared radiometers	Reduced IR signature aircraft
Fiber-optics system	Aircraft/missile onboard communications systems
Air-to-air documents	New air-to-air missile
General-purpose naval and antisubmarine warfare	
Aircraft carrier steam catapult design documents	Aircraft launching system for new aircraft carrier
US MK 48 Torpedo documents	Antisubmarine torpedo
Gamma radiation radiometer	Nuclear submarine wake-detection trailing system
Acoustic spectrum analyzer	Submarine quieting
Powerful coustical vibrator	Submarine and ship sonars
Space and antisatellite weapons	
Documents on systems and heat shielding of the US space shuttle	Reusable space system
Transit naval navigation hardware	First-generation space-based naval radionavigational system
USNAVSTAR navigation system documents	Digital signal processing for counterpart satellite system
High-energy chemical laser documents	Space-based laser weapon
System 101 processing equipment	Digital processing and video for space-based reconnaissance; missile bomb, and remotely piloted vehicle command guidance
Tactical forces	
International radar conference documents	Synthetic aperture radar for aircraft detection
Ground support equipment for US TOW antitank guided missile	Countermeasure system
US Copperhead laser-guided artillery documents	New laser-guided artillery shell
Laser-guided missile documents	Portable antiaircraft system
Infrared imaging subsystem designs	Fire-control system of future tank
Millimeter radar documents	Antitank missile
Pressure measuring instruments and documents	Advanced modeling for new artillery projectiles

Sources: Central Intelligence Agency, *Soviet Acquisition of Militarily Significant Western Technology: An Update,* September, 1985; the Critical Technologies Group, *AMC Guide to Technology Security,* prepared for the Army Materiel Command, November 1987, and made available by the Defense Technology Security Administration.

Under these circumstances, the United States should continue to work with the allies to maintain a stringent system of export controls toward the Soviet Union.

This position is also based on my views of Secretary-General Gorbachev. I agree with the administration that we should want *perestroika* to succeed at home and abroad because success may very well lead to a less aggressive Soviet Union, "restrained in the use of force and less hostile to democracy,"[41] as Secretary Baker said before the Foreign Policy Association on October 16, 1989. My main reservation about Gorbachev has to do less with the public man than with the political forces that will inevitably constrain and shape his actions.

Westerners are just beginning to know Gorbachev, and many of our perceptions of him derive from a well-organized public diplomatic offensive that has catapulted him to the front ranks of popularity. But we should listen to what he is saying as well as to what his colleagues, those who know him far better than we do, have to say. Gorbachev's comments at times suggest he is having great difficulty reconciling his words to the deeds they trigger. As events in Poland, Hungary, Czechoslovakia, and East Germany moved toward multiparty systems, *Pravda* was compelled to write that the party rejected the multiparty system and would maintain the "vanguard" status of the Communist party.[42] Prior to his trip to Lithuania in early January 1990, President Gorbachev characterized the multiparty system as "rubbish."[43]

In his first public comments on the dramatic events in Eastern Europe, he called for the East and West "to meet each other half-way," but warned the West at the same time against exploiting the political turmoil in Eastern Europe to "export capitalism."[44] He added: "When accusations of 'exporting revolution' are replaced with calls for 'exporting capitalism,' we have at hand a dangerous manifestation of old thinking."[45] His threats against the Baltic states should not be taken lightly, particularly because Gorbachev regards the region differently than he does the countries of Central and Eastern Europe. But even here, events appear to reshaping his thinking.

Closer to home, his critics, even those that presumably support him, see him as he is. If Boris Yeltsin's views are somewhat tainted by his alleged personal ambitions to succeed Gorbachev, then perhaps the opinions of Vladislav Starkov, the editor in chief of *Argumenty i Fakty*, are more straightforward. Starkov, who attracted Gorbachev's wrath for publishing "erroneous materials," said, "In the United States, there has been great euphoria. There has been the feeling that so long as Mikhail Gorbachev stays in office we will have democracy and *glasnost*. That is a big mistake. Look at the course he is taking."[46] Gorbachev appears to be taking two courses: one of glasnost abroad and one of "democratic centralism" at home. A careful reading of his book *Perestroika* (which, until he repudiates it, remains a valid reflection of his thinking) leads me to conclude that Gorbachev demonstrably remains a product of the same party system that spawned Lenin, Stalin, Nikita Khrushchev, and Brezhnev. Gorbachev's position reminds me of something Winston Churchill said upon his assumption of power during the war: "I have no intention of overseeing the dissolution of the British empire." I do not believe that Gorbachev took over the reins of power to oversee the dissolution of the Soviet empire or the Communist party he leads. I suspect he will use whatever means are at his disposal to ensure the national security of the Soviet Union and the party's primacy. Gorbachev may not be our enemy, but neither is he yet our friend.

Arrive at a Policy Regarding Joint Ventures. I share the misgiving of those who believe that the Soviet Union views joint ventures as part of its program to acquire Western technology *legally*. However, there is no justification for the obstacles raised by those who would prevent benign, nonstrategic and noncontrolled technologies from being included in U.S.-Soviet joint ventures. It can only be in our long-term interest to assist in the development of market economic principles and the export of Western culture and economic thinking to the Soviet Union.

The executive branch should arrive at a policy to help the Soviet Union restructure its economy toward free-market principles based on the President's and Secretary Baker's suggestion that the United States may be able to offer technical economic assistance. This "policy," announced before the Senate Finance Committee on October 4, 1989, and reiterated at the conclusion of the Malta summit, should serve as the vehicle to get under way, finally, a sound debate within the administration and between the administration and the Congress on the question of the extent to which the U.S. government is prepared to see Gorbachev's economic reforms "succeed," as Secretary Baker said.

Grant Most-Favored-Nation Trading Status Now. The Soviet Union is exceeding Jackson-Vanik restrictions beyond expectation. The administration should grant the Soviet Union most-favored-nation status now and not continue to insist that the Soviets codify emigration policies as a precondition. Their new emigration law will almost certainly not permit completely free emigration, and it is inevitable that sooner or later a meritorious case will arise from our point of view that will not fall within their law. At that point we could find ourselves in the awkward position of urging the Soviets to bypass the very law we insisted they write. It may be better to rely on their administrative policy and the flexibility inherent in it, while at the same time maintaining the annual Jackson-Vanik review and waiver process to guarantee close oversight of their actual practice.

Call for an End to the Soviet Technology Theft Programs. This issue should be placed on the agenda of the upcoming summit. Soviet illegal acquisition programs are legitimate barriers to technology transfer and justification for continued export control restrictions by the United States and COCOM.[47] Failure to solve this problem will make it impossible to upgrade Soviet technology levels via Western assistance.

The Warsaw Pact

Brezhnev Doctrine no, Sinatra Doctrine si.

--Gennadi Gerasimov, Soviet spokesman,
on the new doctrine for Central and
Eastern European political reforms

Perestroika and *glasnost* have had a profound and immediate political impact on Eastern Europe. In April 1989, the labor-led organization Solidarity was legalized in Poland. In June Poland's voters soundly defeated every Communist candidate whom any non-Communist was allowed to challenge. Polish President Wojciech Jaruzelski, facing a choice between force and the voice of the people, opted to permit the formation of a Solidarity-led government, presumably with the public support of Soviet Secretary-General Gorbachev in the process.

In May, Hungarians began prodemocracy demonstrations and in September opened their borders to tens of thousands of East Germans seeking refuge in the West. In October, the Hungarian government formally declared the country a democracy after forty-one years of Communist rule.

In November, soon after a half million East Germans marched in cold rain in Leipzig demanding democracy and freedom, the government dismissed most of the existing ossified leader, including party chief Honecker, and lifted travel restrictions to West Germany. The fast-changing political scene in East Germany culiminated in the dissolution of one of the most rigid Communist regimes and reunification with West Germany.

In Bulgaria, hundreds of thousands of ethnic Turks fled to Turkey; on November 3, 1989, thousands of Bulgarians shouting "democracy" and "*glasnost*" held their first public demonstration in forty years. Veteran Communist leader Todor Zhivkov was dismissed.

In Czechoslovakia, hundreds of thousands of profreedom demonstrators forced the party give up its legally guaranteed leadership role in the government. The government promised free multiparty elections as it booted out five of the six party officials closely associated with the crackdown of the "Prague Spring" in 1968.   Milos Jakes, who was responsible for orchestrating the purge that led to the removal of nearly a half million reformers within the party was the key Communist party official replaced.   The November 25, 1989, events also vindicated and rehabilitated Alexander Dubcek, the ousted former party chief who led the 1968 reform movement.

Between Poland and Czechoslovakia, the political revolutions had been bloodless. Stalinist Romania changed this. When the revolution came to Romania, President Nicolae Ceausescu set loose his loyal security guard, which killed thousands of Romanian citizens.   On December 25, Ceausescu and his wife were in turn executed.   In a bizarre twist of events during the unrest, the U.S. government had signaled Moscow that the United States would not object to Warsaw Pact forces intervening in Romania to bring about peace.

U.S. Technology Transfer Initiatives:
The Case of Poland and Hungary

In any economic and financial aid package to Eastern Europe, technology transfer programs promise to be the most difficult to accommodate.   Not surprisingly, President Bush's April 17, 1989, foreign policy speech at Hamtramck, Michigan, and the President's subsequent visit to Eastern Europe failed to produce any technology transfer provisions in the financial aid package to Poland and Hungary.

Congressional support for administration efforts to assist Poland and Hungary is unanimous. All of the various aid proposals contain elements to address critical needs--especially funds for short-term economic stabilization and food assistance. The proposals also allocate seed money for the development of private-sector joint ventures between Americans and Poles and Hungarians. This will help transfer the most valuable aid of all, working knowledge of free enterprise for people who have been stifled for decades by central control. The aid proposals also contain other key elements to increase contacts between the United States and Poland and Hungary.   They allocate funds to support scientific and environmental programs, to support development of free labor markets and democratic political institutions, and to create an export market for U.S. goods and services.

All these provisions will, for a relatively modest cost, promote a key U.S. objective in Eastern Europe: to make the countries of the area independent, prosperous, and more closely tied to the United States and the West. This is not foreign aid so much as a direct investment in U.S.

security and peace in a region that has been the focus of world confrontation since before World War I.

But U.S. government money is not a panacea for what ails Poland and Hungary. Their problems are systemic. Both have bureaucracies set up to administer socialist planning, not free-market economies. Both are suffering from inflation, Poland certainly more than Hungary. Both suffer from structural problems that will require additional resources if their economies are to be transformed. Poland's foreign debt is nearly $40 billion, Hungary's about $12 billion.

It is crucial that Poland and Hungary's economic structural problems be resolved. I firmly believe, as Felix G. Rohatyn observes, that "the key to real economic change [in Poland and Hungary] will be privatizations of state enterprises, joint ventures and other infusions of Western capital and management."[48]   For example, I strongly endorse General Electric's proposed $150 million investment in Hungary to upgrade technology at Tungsram Company, which makes residential, automotive, and industrial bulbs and has annual sales of $300 million. GE will own 50 percent plus one share of the company and have an option to buy 30 percent more in the future.

Limited to mediocre technology, neither country can hope to develop a competitive, Westernized economy. A Hungarian official told me that they cannot have a first-rate economy with third-rate technology and cannot earn the currency required to transform their backward economy into a modern one if they cannot compete in the world marketplace. Both countries have taken small but important steps to restructure their economies to attract Western capital. Both, for example, permit up to 100 percent ownership of joint ventures and the repatriation of profits. Western investment is inevitably accompanied by Western standards of quality and Western methods of doing business. If the goal of the United States is to wean these economies away from socialism and dependence on the Soviet Union, then an expansion of private-sector investment is the best way to achieve it.

There are, however, some legitimate concerns with Poland and Hungary's close military cooperation with other Warsaw Pact countries, their membership in the Council for Mutual Economic Assistance (CMEA), their illegal technology acquisition and diversion programs, and the continued presence of the KGB in both countries. These are serious problems that cannot be overlooked. But they are not insurmountable obstacles that should cause us to abandon the effort; rather, we should focus on finding ways to encourage Poland and Hungary to continue to seek methods of stabilizing their economies (for example, by bringing inflation under control) and then to transform and integrate them into the world's free marketplace.

Let's be clear about the options we face. The choice is not between holding the line for the status quo or rushing headlong into the unprotected transfer of technology to Warsaw Pact nations. In fact, neither is a real option.

The Heinz Amendment. During the Senate debate on the Poland-Hungarian economic assistance aid package, I proposed an amendment that firmly leaves the horse ahead of the cart. The amendment was driven by the conviction that Poland and Hungary's economies will succeed mainly on the strength of private direct investments. It is my desire to contribute to the development of an environment conducive to private-sector, not government, investments and activity.

As enacted, the amendment read:

> Sec. 702. Report on Confidence Building Measures by Poland and Hungary. Not later than 180 days after the enactment of this Act, the President shall submit a report to the Congress identifying (1) the confidence building measures Poland and Hungary could undertake to facilitate the negotiations of agreements, including bilateral customs and technology transfer agreements, that would encourage greater direct private sector investment in that country; and (2) the confidence building measures Poland and Hungary could undertake with respect to the treatment accorded those countries under the Export Administration Act of 1979.[49]

The same should have been proposed for Czechoslovakia, which was the first Eastern European country to have both a non-Communist president and prime minister.

It is important that the administration take this initial step now--*on its own behalf*--so that we will have a policy with clear markers that will lead to mutually beneficial results. This initiative is crucial for two reasons, one commercial and the other political. First, both countries have identified a wide range of projects that will require capital and higher levels of technology to complete. Second, the United States runs the risk of having other COCOM member states negotiating the ground rules for the transfer of U.S. technology. It would be a serious setback for our geopolitical objectives as well as U.S. commercial interests if the United States failed to include technology transfer programs in future economic assistance plans.

A Three-Point Proposal. Private-sector direct investments in Poland and Hungary (and now Czechoslovakia) will invariably require the transfer of technologies, whether controlled or not. In the event that these countries establish the necessary confidence-building measures to permit a change in our policy, it is in the best interests of the U.S. government to look ahead to the construction of a technology transfer *structure* with *verifiable* elements.

With the expectation that Poland and Hungary will endeavor to foster the required confidence-building measures, I submitted the following three-point technology transfer proposal to Secretaries Baker and Mosbacher as an example of the kind of forward thinking that will be required of current and future administrations. The proposal was intended to establish a dialogue between Congress and the administration on the elements of a structure to safeguard the transfer of Western technology to Poland and Hungary. The structure would include a technology "differential" not unlike the early China green-zone levels, a customs-to-customs agreement, and a strategic trade agreement containing certain elements approved under COCOM's Third Country Initiative.

The first part of the structure is the strategic trade differential. The United States already differentiates exports to Poland and Hungary from those to the remaining members of the Warsaw Pact. Poland and Hungary are under country group "W," whereas the Soviet Union and other Warsaw Pact members are under country group "Z." China (and Yugoslavia) are in country group "V." The significance of the country groups is mainly symbolic, but they do say something about U.S. policy toward the country groups. For example, few would argue that prior to the Tiananmen massacre, U.S. technology transfer policy was both symbolically and substantively different toward China than toward other countries on the COCOM control lists.

The creation of a differential takes time--as long as two years (provided, of course, that the China green line is not extended immediately, a decision I would advocate and support). The United States must first determine the levels of technology under the differential and must then negotiate it with its COCOM partners. (The latter is in keeping with the administration's policy of seeking a joint approach toward Poland and Hungary.)

It took over five years for the United States and COCOM to agree on the China green zone categories. But the Chinese knew well in advance that the United States was leading the effort to liberalize the COCOM control lists, and until the recent suppression of student demonstrators occurred, the United States and COCOM reaped the economic and political benefits of the liberalization exercise. In 1980 the levels of technology allowed to be exported to China and the Soviet bloc were essentially identical. Today, they are not.

Given the environment created by *perestroika*, negotiating a differential in COCOM should not be difficult, and it can be done expeditiously. The challenge may well be to rein in the willingness to liberalize at levels comparably higher than China at the same point in time. The globalization and commoditization of high technology has allowed the Soviet Union and the bloc to acquire or develop more sophisticated technology products than were available to China ten or even five years ago.

The vexing question is what assurances will the United States and COCOM have that neither Poland nor Hungary will divert these technologies to the Soviet Union, other Warsaw Pact members, or other non-COCOM or non-COCOM-cooperating countries? The answer is that the United States and COCOM cannot be totally assured that diversions will not occur.

However, my proposal still requires individually validated licenses. Both countries have good records in protecting technology acquired legally, which includes civil aircraft and advanced computers. These exports were approved after an exhaustive interagency review to determine that the exports were for commercial or civil use and had no clearly identified direct military application. This case-by-case approach is a reflection of Poland and Hungary's country group classification. The lure to obtain Western technology legally may make it possible to negotiate the second and third parts of a technology transfer safeguard structure: the customs-to-customs agreement and a strategic trade agreement. These two types of agreements are first and foremost acts of political willingness, and only second are they related to trade. Both agreements contain extraterritorial aspects, but I expect the other governments to be willing to pay that price.

Regarding the customs agreement, the United States has concluded ten such agreements, with another eight in various stages of negotiations, including one with Yugoslavia. Customs is contemplating at least five agreements, including one with Hungary, Czechoslovakia and Poland.

A customs-to-customs memorandum of understanding (MOU) would provide for a mutual assistance agreement to prevent, investigate, and repress breaches of customs laws. It is a mechanism below treaty status that establishes a legal basis for one country's customs authorities to act on assistance requests of another country. Challenged and upheld in U.S. courts, this legal basis rests on a model agreement of the Customs Cooperation Council (CCC). (The CCC is a formal organization of 104 nations that study customs issues and attempt to resolve customs problems). Through membership in the CCC, both Poland and Hungary have already informally cooperated with the United States, mainly in drug and commercial fraud areas.

One problem with customs-to-customs MOUs is that they do not provide for any verification that the requests are being conducted completely and accurately by the host country's customs service. This gap is filled by the third part of the proposal, strategic trade agreement (STA). STAs contain several elements approved by COCOM under its Third Country Initiative. The United States has negotiated or is in the process of negotiating these agreements with such diverse countries as India, Pakistan, Israel, South Korea, Singapore, Taiwan, Malaysia, Indonesia, Finland, Switzerland, Austria, and Sweden.

One key provision of the STA is the prelicense-postshipment check that permits the Department of Commerce to verify that an export has arrived at the destination listed in the end-use certificate attached to the export license. Commerce--either through its Office of Export Enforcement agents or Foreign Commercial Service attachés assigned to embassies--is permitted to conduct random inspections to make sure that the equipment is located where the importer says it will be located unless prior authorization from the United States allowed reexportation or internal relocation. In addition, the STA includes the import certificate-delivery verification system. As mentioned in Chapter 2, these two documents were adopted by COCOM in the early 1950s and are issued by the importing government to protect against fraud and diversion by its businesspeople.

The United States currently utilizes an end-use certificate (BXA-629) for exports to Communist countries. Because of the relatively low level of technology exports to the Soviet bloc countries, the verification required is normally done by the receiving company, not by the government. The IC/DV system requires the cooperating government to amend its laws--if necessary--to provide penalties for violations of its export control laws and, in the case of the United States, reexport provisions.

STAs also include restrictions against reexporting U.S. technologies without the authorization of Commerce. Finally, STAs include enforcement provisions to allow U.S. Customs to investigate violations of U.S. export controls in the receiving country. This extraterritorial aspect of the STA is generally the most difficult to negotiate, but it has been done with greater frequency than believed possible. The customs agreement and the STA are mutually compatible; STAs are flexible in both form and substance.

COCOM and the Polish-Hungarian Technology Transfer Question. The Bush Administration's initial response to the three-point proposal was lukewarm if not cold. The administration's argument rested mainly on Poland's and Hungary's military status within the Warsaw Pact. However, pressure from domestic interests and several COCOM countries to extend to Poland and Hungary "the lighter COCOM treatment accorded to China . . . in recognition of the democratic progress"[50] in the two countries succeeded in placing the issue squarely on the agenda of the COCOM high-level meeting October 25-26, 1989. According to the *London Financial Times*, "Washington reacted cooly to this challenge to its traditional leadership in COCOM." The problem, the *Times* concluded, "is that the Europeans, keen to sell into the Eastern bloc's huge market, appear to believe in liberalization first and fence-building second [i.e., improving their enforcement systems], while the United States wants a strictly 'parallel' approach. All this may have brought COCOM . . . near deadlock."[51]

The Future of the Warsaw Pact

It is presumptuous at this point to predict the future of NATO and the Warsaw Pact. The unilateral reductions announced by President Gorbachev certainly augur well for a reduced threat by Warsaw Pact conventional forces to Western Europe and the United States. NATO is also undergoing an internal assessment of its own force reductions, aided in no small measure by President Bush's reductions announced at the Brussels summit in June 1989.

There are, perhaps, some hopeful signs that the Warsaw Pact is in the process of evolving from a purely offensive military organization to a political-military defense structure. In April 1987, during a visit to Prague, Gorbachev hinted that Moscow would put aside the Brezhnev Doctrine of tight control over the Warsaw Pact members and eventually adopt what his Foreign Ministry spokesman, Gennadi Gerasimov, recently described as "the Sinatra doctrine," letting each state do it "my way."

On July 9, 1989, the Warsaw Pact leaders concluded their annual meeting in Bucharest by affirming the right of member states to decide their own pace of reform and pledging to work for additional agreements with NATO to reduce conventional and nuclear arms. The pact's final communiqué proposed to create a "center for lessening the military threat and preventing surprise attacks in Europe."[52] The communiqué also affirmed the right of the pact's member nations to decide their own futures and further stated, "There are no universal models of socialism . . . . No country has the right to dictate events in another country, to assume the position of a judge or arbiter," a theme Gorbachev had earlier announced in Prague.[53]

On November 26, Soviet Foreign Minister Eduard Shevardnadze visited Poland a month after the Solidarity-led government took office. Shevardnadze's visit overlapped with a meeting of foreign ministers of the Warsaw Pact nations. Speaking of the future orientation of the Warsaw Pact, he said the military aspect should be deemphasized in favor of a more "political" defense agreement. In the future, he added, the security of the pact should be resolved "through political measures."[54]

The Polish government added its own wish list. According to a government spokesman, Poland wants the Warsaw Pact to make a distinction between the Soviet "zone of security" in Poland and its "sphere of influence."[55] The Polish government proposed to remain within the Soviet security sphere but did not want to be considered within the Soviet sphere of influence. The latter is an important distinction: It justifies Soviet interference in the domestic affairs of the Warsaw Pact members. Although the Soviet government has not gone as far as Poland would like, Shevardnadze did pledge not to interfere in Poland's internal affairs. So far, the Soviet government has kept its pledge.

Several confidence-building measures are currently under way that U.S. analysts say raise "new questions about the viability of the Warsaw Pact as a cohesive, effective military alliance."[56] For example:

- Poland, Hungary, Czechoslovakia, and Bulgaria have announced their intention to reduce military spending by 25 percent in 1991.
- Poland, Czechoslovakia, and Hungary have declared that their approval must be given before military forces can be used outside national territory.
- The Czech government has asked Moscow to remove an estimated 75,000 troops from Czechoslovakia by the end of 1990.
- Hungary, Czechoslovakia, and Romania have ordered that pledges of fealty to the Communist party be stripped from military service oaths.
- A new wave of antimilitarism is sweeping through Eastern Europe.[56]

In addition to these military initiatives, Eastern Europe's drive for independence from Soviet domination has had a notable effect on the economic relationship between Moscow and the Council for Mutual Economic Assistance. On January 9-10, 1990, the ten member nations of CMEA agreed to move toward a market-based system of free trade yet keep certain controls. Hungary and Czechoslovakia, however, opposed the preservation of some controls and proposed instead to eviscerate CMEA immediately to allow its members the freedom to negotiate bilateral trade agreements both East and West.[57]

China

He who ties the knot, unties it.

> --Chinese proverb cited by Chinese leader
> Deng Xiaoping, referring to the imposition of
> U.S. sanctions after the Tiananmen massacre

The Nixon Administration opened China to U.S. trade opportunities in 1972, but the substantive liberalization of export controls occurred during the Carter and Reagan Administrations. In 1980, after a high-level mission to China, the Carter Administration announced a further liberalization of dual-use exports to China and, more importantly, accepted a munitions wish list from the Chinese that was to serve as the basis for the military cooperation program under the Reagan Administration. The so-called China card had entered the geopolitical game in Asia.

Beginning in 1981, the Reagan Administration engaged in a wide-ranging interagency review of U.S. export control policy and decided to continue the restrictive policy toward the Soviet Union, reinvigorate COCOM, and further liberalize export controls toward China. In effect, the Reagan Administration decided to establish the so-called, China green zones or green lines.

In November 1983 the administration officially introduced new export regulations for the transfer of technology to China. Nearly three and a half years later, the United States formally submitted the China green-zones proposals to COCOM, where they were subsequently incorporated into the COCOM Industrial (Dual-Use) List.

The Green Zones

The changes were significant. The United States and COCOM had agreed to establish parameters for several of the controlled categories using a three-tier differentiated structure. The first level--the green zones--covers COCOM's "administrative exceptions note" level of low-end technologies. This level requires a validated license but carries the presumption of approval by the national capitals after the proper end-use and end-users have been established. Green-zone cases are not referred to COCOM. In the United States, China green-zone cases are routinely approved by the Department of Commerce, and no referral to the Department of Defense is required.

The second level--the yellow, or intermediate, zone--covers a higher level of technology, requires a validated license, carries the presumption of approval, but does not require referral to COCOM except through monthly statistical reports. Within the U.S. interagency process, however, these cases are referred to the Department of Defense. The third level-- the red zone--generally includes items in the six military offensive mission areas (discussed in the following section), requires a validated license, carries the presumption of denial, and calls for mandatory referral to COCOM (and Defense). The latter stringent requirements, as we shall see, have never discouraged the United States from submitting more "general exceptions" cases than other COCOM members.

U.S. and COCOM Export Control Policy Before Tiananmen

The United States' and COCOM's liberal China export control policy notwithstanding, China is retained on the proscribed lists because China, according to official U.S. policy, has strategic capabilities unlike those of other friendly countries. Although this policy statement has never been elaborated, U.S. export control policy permits transfers of dual-use and munitions equipment and technologies restricted to conventional defensive capabilities and reviews exports on a case-by-case basis with the presumption of denial in the following six mission areas: nuclear weapons and delivery systems, intelligence gathering, electronic warfare, antisubmarine warfare, power projection, and air superiority. If the proposed export falls outside of these areas, it is fair game, as the figures below show. Unlike exports to the Soviet Union or the Warsaw Pact countries, U.S. and COCOM export control policies--up to the time of the June 1989 suppression of prodemocracy activities--permitted the approval of cases even when the end-user or end-use was military or even if the export could have contributed to Chinese military development.

COCOM has generally followed the U.S. lead in liberalizing export controls toward China, but COCOM members, as the United States itself, succumbed to China's all-out and highly successful public relations campaign to convince world leaders of its political stability. The Chinese also stressed their commitment to economic modernization, which in time succeeded in attracting vast sums of foreign investment and credits from several COCOM countries. In 1988 and 1989, for example, seven COCOM countries had offered China nearly $8 billion in credits. (See Table 3.3.)

Let there be no doubt: Chinese leaders successfully convinced Western leaders of the irreversibility of China's opening to the West. Not surprisingly, then, before the Tiananmen massacre of prodemocracy student demonstrators, there was growing evidence that some COCOM members were preparing to change the rules with or without U.S. acquiescence. The United States, itself caught up in China's economic reform program, chose to cooperate in still a fifth liberalization meeting scheduled just prior to Tiananmen. The massacre stopped the further trade liberalization dead in its tracks just as it stopped the democracy movement in China.

U.S. and COCOM Export Control Policy Since Tiananmen

"A Big Chill," former U.S. Ambassador Winston Lord writes, "has descended over China."[58] Put another way, U.S.-Chinese relations have been in a state of suspension since June 5. Shortly after the Tiananmen

TABLE 3.3
Concessional and Mixed Credits to China, 1988-1989 (in millions of U.S. dollars)

	Amount	Date Offered	Period	Comment
Japan	6,000	1988	1989-1995	Concessional from OECD for 41 projects
United Kingdom	540	1988	1988-1990	Mixed credit
Canada	280	1988	1989-1990	Concessional
Spain	450	1989	1989-1991	Mixed credit. Replenishes $300 million, 19986-1988
Australia	160	1988	1989-1991	Mixed credit
West Germany	122	1989	1989	Concessional
West Germany	250	1989	1989	Mixed credits for Shanghai subway
Sweden	100	1989	1989	Mixed credits

Source: U.S.-China Business Council. Unpublished data.

massacre, the United States and several COCOM members announced a variety of measures to demonstrate their condemnation of the Chinese government's brutal policy of suppression. On June 5, President Bush announced a program of sanctions against China that was followed by similar actions by other Western governments. The U.S. program of suspensions originally included:

1. the suspension of all government-to-government sales of commercial export of weapons;
2. the suspension of visits between U.S. and Chinese military leaders;
3. sympathetic review of requests by Chinese students in the United States to extend their visas;
4. the offer of humanitarian and medical assistance, through the Red Cross, to those injured during the assault;
5. review of other aspects of the bilateral relationship as events in China unfolded.

The fifth point, we now know, hid a number of additional sanctions that the executive order did not make clear. Hidden underneath the "other aspects of the bilateral relationship," was the President's decision to suspend further liberalization of export controls toward China. President Bush, in the careful style of diplomacy that marks his brand of leadership, instructed the State Department quietly to propose to COCOM the postponement of the China liberalization meeting then under way (the proposal accepted unanimously), suspend a license for jetliners destined for China that contained controlled equipment (the license was eventually granted), and postpone a license application for the launch of a U.S. satellite by China. Green-zone (dual-use) cases that were being processed before Tiananmen were held up temporarily for review but with the presumption of approval when the review was completed.

Publicly, the Congress jumped on the apparent omission of a ban on technology exports to China, as well as China's human rights violations and U.S. financial assistance to China under a number of national and international organizations. Within days, a large number of bills were introduced in the Congress to fill the presumed loopholes. The student problem attracted the greatest attention initially: Congress introduced no fewer than eleven bills in the first week after Tiananmen offering the students some form of refuge in the United States. Other bills contained provisions to halt U.S. financial assistance to China by such international and national financial institutions as the World Bank, the Overseas Protection Insurance Corporation (OPIC), ExIm Bank, and AID's Trade Development Program (TDP). A few touched on China's human rights abuses, mainly calling for Tibet's independence from China. In the House, an amendment containing a panoply of sanctions was approved by 418 to 0 over the opposition of the Bush Administration. In the Senate, a similar measure passed 81 to 10, also over the administration's opposition.

In the latter half of 1989, China disappeared from the front pages of the press, from the House and Senate floors, but not from the quiet and then secret diplomacy of the administration. In late July, Secretary Baker met with the Chinese foreign minister in Paris in a reversal of the administration's policy prohibiting contacts with China's leaders above the rank of assistant secretary. A State Department mid-level officer met in Washington with a Chinese delegation en route to Brussels to discuss China's membership to the GATT, and a Chinese military delegation arrived in the United States to continue preparations for the upgrade of the F-8 jet fighter.

In China, foreign businesses reopened their offices, and, for all intents and purposes, it was business as usual. Reports from China, however, said otherwise. For example, the prestigious China Business Council reported that the "prospects for American companies doing business in China appear to be getting bleaker, not better. . . . Now, for the first time since the China trade was reopened in 1979, the word 'expropriation' has slipped into conversations of Americans with business interests [in China]."[59]

On November 22, Senate and House conferees agreed on a program of legislated sanctions against China, which the Bush administration reluctantly accepted.[60] Title 9 (the China amendment) of the State Department Authorization Bill (H.R. 1487) contained two parts. The first part stated that the suspensions of programs and activities by the President on June 5 *shall continue*. This section was to be binding on the President, but subject to Presidential waiver if the President certifies that the government of the People's Republic of China has made progress on a program of political reform throughout the country or if he finds it in the U.S. national interest to lift the suspension(s).

The second part contained additional measures urging what the President *should* do if the situation in China were not to improve. This part--which included measures concerning the Export-Import Bank, most-favored-nation status, the liberalization of export controls, and the GATT--was not binding. It did reflect, however, the broad agreement of the U.S. public and the U.S. government to take additional measures consistent with U.S. values if China persisted in a systematic violation of basic human rights.

In constructing the amendment in this way, Congress acknowledged the President's request to retain flexibility in the conduct of foreign policy. It also recognized that the President must weigh several elements in determining the national interest, especially human rights and national security considerations. Congress showed its awareness that U.S. economic interests are part of the national interest but that the economic interests of the country and of individual U.S. companies should not be the sole factor in a Presidential determination to apply the national interest waiver.

The President, in any event, vetoed the bill in November 1989 but stipulated reasons other than China. In late January 1990, the conferees approved a new bill, H.R. 3792, which did not contain the objectionable provisions the President vetoed but did contain the China sanctions. The President signed the bill.

Issues in U.S.-China Strategic Trade Relations

Bilateral Trade. U.S.-Chinese bilateral trade has soared in the past ten years, and in a fashion that belies the antagonistic history between the two countries and the historical justification of U.S. (and COCOM) national security export controls toward China. Since China opened its doors to international trade, the United States has reaped significant economic and political benefits from China's economic modernization

TABLE 3.4
U.S.-China Trade, 1981-1988 (in millions of U.S. dollars)

	1981	1982	1983	1984	1985	1986	1987	1988
U.S. exports	3.603	2.912	2.173	3.004	3.852	3.105	3.488	4.757
U.S. imports	2.062	2.502	2.477	3.381	4.224	5.241	6.911	8.379
U.S. trade balance	+1.540	+.410	-.304	-.377	-.373	-2.135	-3.422	-3.622

Source: U.S. Department of Commerce. International Trade Administration. Office of Trade and Investment Analysis.

program. China, too, has benefited from U.S. trade. From 1981 to 1988, U.S.-China bilateral trade has averaged $7.5 billion, with a low of $4.65 billion in 1983 and a high of $13.1 billion in 1988. China has had a trade surplus with the United Staes since 1983, reaching an all-time high of $3.6 billion in 1988. (See Table 3.4.)

China has benefited mainly from direct investment. Hong Kong notwithstanding, the United States ranks first in cumulative direct foreign investment in China, with a total of $3.4 billion, or 12 percent of the total between 1979 and 1988. Before Tiananmen, there were about 350 U.S.-Chinese joint venture projects either operating or in the planning stage. U.S.-Chinese and COCOM-Chinese joint ventures appear to have escaped the fate of U.S.-Soviet joint ventures. The United States and other COCOM members have signed contracts to export billions of dollars in technology and capital equipment, as Table 3.5 illustrates for 1988 alone. In addition, twelve U.S. companies have spent over $1 billion to date searching for oil off the Chinese coast.

Finally, in the area of intellectual capital, there are currently about 40,000 Chinese students studying at U.S. universities, compared to an insignificant number from the Soviet Union, as Table 3.6 illustrates.

Liberalization of Dual-Use Export Controls. Since 1983, when U.S. policy officially characterized U.S. relations with China as "friendly, but not allied," the United States and COCOM have applied the green zones to several commodity categories including computers, computerized instruments, microcircuits, electronic instruments, recording equipment, and semiconductor production equipment. Between 1983 and 1988, approved[61] export licenses rose from 2,834 with a value of $932 million to an all-time high of 8,637 in 1985 with a value of $5.5 billion. In 1988 the United States approved 5,724 licenses with a value of $2.9 billion.

From 1982 to 1988, U.S. exports of dual-use high technology to China have increased from $630 million to $1.72 billion. (See Table 3.7.) In 1988 the U.S. high tech trade surplus with China totaled $816 million, far overshadowing U.S. high tech trade with the Soviet Union and Eastern Europe.

TABLE 3.5
Number and Value of Technology and Capital Equipment Contracts in China, 1988 (in millions of U.S. dollars)

	Number of Contracts	Value
Italy	26	815
France	31	576
Britain	31	437
West Germany	66	419
Japan	81	272
United States	101	256
Other	94	534
Total	430	3,550

Sources: China Daily, Beijing, February 23, 1989, and China Business Council Report, March 23, 1989.

TABLE 3.6
Chinese and Soviet Students in the United States, 1978-1988

	Chinese	Soviet
1988	40,000	< 100
1987	25,170	77
1986	20,030	97
1985	13,980	83
1984	10,100	230
1983	8,140	260
1982	6,230	360
1981	4,350	430
1980	2,770	630
1979	1,000	600
1978	28	170

Source: Washington Times, May 5, 1989. Used with permission.

Finally, the United States usually accounts for the greatest number of general exceptions requests to COCOM. Between 1985 and 1988, the United States submitted 76.2 percent (5,994) of all general exceptions requests to COCOM, followed by the UK with 11.0 percent and Japan with 6.48 percent.

Liberalization in COCOM. As China fared in the United States, so it fared in COCOM. In early 1985 COCOM began detailed consultations to liberalize export controls to China. In December 1985 COCOM drew up guidelines in twenty-seven product categories that would no longer require review. Approval was determined by national capitals, with statistical data provided to COCOM monthly. In 1986 and 1987, five more categories were added to the green zones, to bring to thirty-two the

TABLE 3.7
U.S. High Tech Trade with COCOM-Proscribed Countries, 1979-1988 (rounded to nearest million of U.S. dollars)

	1979	1980	1981	1982	1983	1984	1985	1986	1987	1988
Total U.S exports	43,524	54,712	60,390	58,112	60,158	65,150	68,425	72,517	84,071	104,279
USSR	92	47	56	47	75	62	48	31	83	76
China	220	665	827	634	651	822	1,706	1,275	1,428	1,717
E.Europe[a]	110	155	79	64	64	67	100	113	79	105
% to COCOM-proscribed countries	0.96	1.6	1.6	1.3	1.3	1.4	2.7	1.9	1.9	1.9
Total U.S. imports	23,443	28,015	33,826	34,521	41,397	59,463	64,778	75,107	83,481	98,311
USSR	5	49	15	14	14	4	5	5	17	16
China	12	27	44	56	62	99	114	165	444	901
E. Europe	59	51	45	39	33	42	54	66	57	63
U.S. high tech trade balance[b]	20,081	26,697	26,564	23,591	18,761	6,047	3,647	-2,590	590	5,968
% from COCOM-proscribed countries	0.3	0.4	0.3	0.3	0.2	0.3	0.3	---	0.6	0.9

[a]Eastern Europe's figures do not distinguish between Warsaw Pact and non-Warsaw Pact countries.
[b]Commerce's definition of high tech items is based on the U.S. Standard Industrial Classification (SIC). (The SIC, based on 1972-1977 classes, was revised in January 1988.) The DOC definition includes guided missiles and spacecraft; communications equipment and electronic components; aircraft and parts; office, computing, and accounting machines; ordnance and accessories; drugs and medicines; industrial inorganic chemicals; professional and scientific instruments; engines; turbines; and synthetic resins, rubber, and fibers.

Source: U.S. Department of Commerce.

number of categories liberalized solely for China. In fall 1988 COCOM completed its fourth liberalization of the China green zones. Tiananmen postponed a fifth exercise under way at the time of the massacre.

Two significant results have occurred from the rate and levels of liberalization. First, U.S. and COCOM export control policies toward China are *still* significantly more liberal than those to the Soviet bloc. For example, the green zone for computers has increased eighteenfold in the last five years, from a processing data rate (PDR) of 32 in 1983 (PDR is a COCOM formula to designate the power of computers), to 550 in 1989. The highest PDR level allowed for the Soviet bloc is 78, just below the "no exceptions" level. In operational terms, this means that China can import sophisticated mainframe computers such as the IBM 3090, whereas the Soviet Union can import some old mainframes, some minicomputers, and some PCs below, but not including, the IBM PS/2. Second, the number of license applications in the United States has dropped from the high of 8,637 in 1985 to 5,724 in 1988. Further, the number of exception requests has also dropped from 4,425 in 1985 to 744 in 1988. The drop in license applications and fewer exception requests were caused by China's initial buying spree and subsequent drop in foreign reserves, which forced some belt-tightening measures.

Liberalization of Munitions Export Controls. Since China became eligible for U.S. commercial munitions exports in 1982, the U.S. government has processed over 1,000 license applications valued at over $1 billion and approved sales in excess of $800 million. In 1985 Congress approved the first foreign military sale (FMS) arms program to China for the modernization of large-caliber artillery ammunition production facilities, with letters of agreement (LOA) for $26 million signed in June 1986.

In July 1986 the United States and COCOM also approved the avionics upgrade of the Chinese F-8 defense interceptor, with an LOA for $502 million signed in October. Also in 1986, four Mark Mod-2 torpedoes were approved as end-item sales along with a coproduction project valued at $90 million. Congressional and COCOM review of the sale of AN/TPQ-37 artillery locating radars was approved in February 1987 at a value of $62 million.

COCOM's International Munitions List (IML) governs munitions exports to China and the Soviet bloc. In May 1987 COCOM approved a package to liberalize munitions exports to China, making China, once again, the only proscribed country to receive such treatment in the control lists. The package covered thirteen categories; the liberalization parameters were generally for defensive and ground forces-oriented military equipment at least one generation behind U.S. military capabilities and not incorporating technology less than seven (and, in some cases, ten) years old.

The selected items that were liberalized included such categories as small arms and machine guns, large-caliber armaments, ammunition, bombs, torpedoes, rockets and guided and unguided missiles, tanks and vehicles, defensive equipment for use against toxicological agents, military explosives, vessels of war and special naval equipment, aircraft and helicopters, special armored equipment, and military infrared and thermal-imaging equipment.

In 1986 COCOM considered seventy-five munitions cases, fifty of which were submitted by the United States alone. Only three cases were denied. The dollar value for all the cases totaled $798 million, with the United States accounting for $697 million of the total. (Figures are not available for more recent years).

U.S. Foreign Policy Controls. As noted, the United States and its COCOM partners had their first difference of opinion regarding the use of export controls as an instrument of U.S. foreign policy toward China in 1956-1957 over the China differential. Despite the flurry of liberalization trends favorable to China, the China meetings continue to take place in a heated and acrimonious environment. Although the United States has for national security reasons blocked some liberalization proposals (such as the proposal to allow the export of intercity, common-channel signaling telecommunications equipment), it has also blocked liberalization in other areas for foreign policy reasons not related to Western national security interests.[62] China's arms export policies have been the primary focus of foreign policy controls toward China.

For example in fall 1987, despite protests from COCOM, the United States succeeded in postponing a scheduled meeting to liberalize export controls to China after evidence of Iran's use of Chinese Silkworm missiles in the Persian Gulf was confirmed. When China agreed to halt the sale of Silkworms to Iran, the meeting resumed, leading to another round of significant liberalization. Perceptions, we know, can often be more powerful than reality, and the perception in COCOM, despite hard evidence to the contrary, was that the United States was using COCOM for its own foreign policy ends.

At the meeting in progress at the time of the Tiananmen massacre, COCOM was on the verge of creating still another difference of opinion. The issue was removing China from the control lists. In 1988 some COCOM members had floated a trial balloon to remove China from the proscribed list. Although nothing happened, the marker was placed, and still another stringent export control was challenged. Some COCOM members also recommended drawing up a shorter but highly restrictive red-zone control list to replace the vastly liberalized green-zone list. The COCOM members argued that such a shorter control list would reduce COCOM's work load even more and expedite the review process significantly. Before the first liberalization, it was not uncommon for COCOM to take from six months to a year to review China cases; today it takes about six weeks. After the fourth liberalization round, COCOM set its aim at a four-week turnaround time, a treatment not accorded to West-West licenses generally by the U.S. interagency review system.

China and the 1988 Omnibus Trade Bill. China's fingerprints are all over the export control provisions of the 1988 Omnibus Trade and Competitiveness Bill. The most significant provision benefiting China trade was the establishment of a distribution license for China. The trade bill clearly made the distribution license an "exception" for China not available to other controlled countries.

The act also called for using the China green zones as the cutoff level for exports to COCOM and COCOM-cooperating countries under a new general license, G-COCOM (no authorization required; no document issued). These controlled categories still require an individual validated license for exports to China, but given the pace of liberalization since 1985, it would have been only a matter of time before China would have been granted the same general license now available to COCOM and COCOM-cooperating third countries. The Chinese government shot more than its citizens in Tiananmen Square; it shot itself in the foot.

The Future of U.S.-Chinese Relations

Before Tiananmen, the United States sought a relationship with China built on the broad compatibility of mutual strategic interests that contributed to stability in Asia. China's rapprochement with the Soviet Union did not change the basis of that assessment. Indeed, the United States publicly welcomed the rapprochement. There were, however, a number of significant differences between the United States and China that would have tested the durability of the relationship in the next decade. These differences remain in limbo, but they are worth reviewing.

At the sixth session of the U.S.-China Joint Commission on Commerce and Trade (JCCT), which met in Washington May 9-11, 1988--the last bilateral trade meeting between the two countries before Tiananmen--the results were disappointing. The U.S. annual status report concluded that although the evolution of U.S. and multilateral export control policies had been an important symbol of the growing trust between the two countries, major disagreements served to keep China on the "potential enemy" list. The most significant differences included:

1. the sale of arms sales to Iran, particularly antiship missiles, and use of Silkworm missiles against U.S. ships in the Gulf (Despite the cessation of Silkworm sales, Iran remains China's largest buyer of conventional arms. After the Tiananmen Square incident, reports began to circulate of the possible resumption of Chinese sales of M-9 missiles to the Middle East);

2. the sale of CSS-2 intermediate-range ballistic missiles to Saudi Arabia (Despite assurances from China that the missiles will not be

equipped with nuclear warheads, the danger of missile proliferation in the Middle East is increasing);

3. human rights violations in Tibet (This issue has led to intense friction between the United States and China, on a par with U.S. human rights friction with the Soviet Union. With or without Tiananmen, the issue contained the potential for linking human rights to trade restrictions in much the same way that previous Soviet restrictive emigration policies served to suspend U.S.-Soviet bilateral trade relations.);

4. China's refusal to declare a nonaggression policy toward Taiwan (The United States, in turn, continues to sell U.S. arms to Taiwan under the Taiwan Relations Act, which the PRC considers interference in its internal domestic affairs.);

5. China's population planning programs (Alleged abuses by the Chinese in abortions and involuntary sterilization programs have led to the withdrawal, at U.S. insistence, of significant funds from the United Nations Fund for Population Activities (UNFPA) as well as the Agency for International Development (AID). The Bush Administration threatened to veto any bill that contained funds for UNFPA earmarked for China.);

6. continued Chinese barriers to a healthy investment climate (Various international financial institutions have warned China of the need to remove trade barriers and currency restrictions, improve the growing number of complicated business taxes, and fill the gap in national treatment of labor, access to inputs, pricing and marketing.);

7. continued failure to protect adequately intellectual property rights, which have led to significant losses, particularly in the area of computer software (The PRC is one of eight countries on the U.S. "priority watch list" for piracy of copyrights, patents, and other intellectual property that costs the U.S. economy tens of billions of dollars and thousands of jobs every year.[63]);

8. on the U.S. side, antiquated laws that discriminate against China on the basis of its past association with the Soviet Union, such as the refusal to extend Generalized System of Preferences (GSP) treatment to China, U.S. requirements for annual MFN reviews, and, of course, inclusion on the COCOM-proscribed lists; and

9. the inability of both countries to bring to a conclusion negotiations on a bilateral investment treaty started in 1983 to bolster U.S. investment in China (One of the obstacles to a BIT between the two countries has been China's refusal to sign an agreement that contained a provision to pay full costs in the event of a political reversal in China that led to the nationalization or expropriation of

U.S. business interests in China. If and when the U.S. and China resume negotiations to restore any semblance of the past relationship, the conclusion of the BIT, with a provision to protect against nationalization or expropriation, would be a necessary condition to further progress in the relationship.)

China as a National Security Threat Post-Tiananmen. During the negotiations between Congress and the White House over the final wording of the proposed sanctions against China, the administration scored a victory that, in principle, gave the president the flexibility and tools to salvage the U.S.-Chinese relationship. At White House insistence, the China amendment preserved the President's right to waive the sanctions if he deemed it "in the national interest." The conferees rejected House language that would have permitted the President to lift the sanctions only "in the national *security* interest," a far narrower and tougher standard to impose. The President vetoed the bill, but for reasons not related to China.

The significance of the compromise language between the executive and legislative branches cannot be underestimated for the future of U.S.-Chinese relations. Granted, the world expressed its abhorrence and condemnation for what happened in Tiananmen in June 1989. It is variously estimated that between 700 and 1,000 people died, and thousands more were arrested and jailed. The lives of foreigners residing in Beijing and other larger cities were clearly imperiled. Foreign businesses closed their offices and fled the country. Ambassadors were recalled. The Chinese government imposed martial law, and the army is still a major presence in the larger cities. "The most cold-blooded observer," writes Ambassador Lord, "would have difficulty justifying the Chinese government's policies since June."[64]

The deepest meaning of Tiananmen for China's relations with the West, therefore, is that its actions did not lead and have not led, to the best of my knowledge, to a reassessment of China as a threat to the national security of the United States and its allies. This, more than any other single salient factor, may be the only remaining--and redeeming--piece of the relationship left with the United States and COCOM member states that can serve as the basis for rebuilding it. The prospect of restoring normalcy to the bilateral relationship, however, will depend on the PRC's finding the concrete means--the replacement of the main advocates of the massacre with leaders not connected to it, for example--of signaling its own reappraisal of the events leading up to and including the Tiananmen massacre.

Unilateral Moves to Improve the Bilateral Relationship. The Bush

Administration has taken unilateral actions that reveal the extent to which it is prepared to go to maintain the relationship. On December 10, 1989, the President announced that his national security adviser and the deputy secretary of state had paid a surprise visit to Beijing to bring "new impetus and vigor" into U.S.-Chinese relations to overcome the deterioration that had occurred in the aftermath of the Tiananmen incident.[65] The announcement produced immediate criticism in the press and Congress.[66] Then, on December 18, the White House dropped another bombshell: the admission of still another, secret trip to Beijing one month after the incident.[67] The President justified both visits by citing his desire not to isolate China from world affairs.[68]

As a measure of this commitment, on December 19 the President announced his decision to authorize the issuance of three licenses for the export of U.S. communications satellites to China (embargoed by the Congress) and to permit new lending by the ExIm Bank for China (also banned by the Congress).[69] By these actions, the President inadvertently established the veracity of the Chinese proverb, quoted at the beginning of this section, which the Chinese cite to blame the United States for the consequences of Tiananmen.

The administration's single most important and controversial action to maintain the relationship, however, was the veto of the Chinese Student Status Immigration Act (H.R. 2712). On June 6, the President ordered the attorney general to provide certain protections to Chinese students by deferring the enforced departure of Chinese nationals because of their involvement in the prodemocracy activities in the United States prior to and after the Tiananmen incident. The Congress passed a bill to afford essentially the same protections as in the President's executive order. Arguing that the executive order went further in protecting the students *and other Chinese* than the bill did, and that the executive order "preserv[ed]" his "ability to manage foreign relations," the President vetoed the bill. On January 24, the House overrode the veto (390 to 5), but on January 25, the Senate sustained it (62 to 37).

In the weeks preceding the vote on the Chinese student bill, China lifted martial law in some, but not all, of China's major cities, released nearly 600 people arrested for their involvement in the Tiananmen activities, allowed a Voice of America (VOA) correspondent to return to China (but did not stop jamming VOA), and removed the armed guards surrounding the U.S. embassy in Beijing. Notably missing from China's unilateral moves was any mention of the fate of the Chinese dissident Fang Lizhi, who sought asylum in the U.S. embassy and who remained at the embassy well into 1990, when he was finally allowed to leave.

Policy Recommendation. The President has won Congressional support, including my own, for his China policy in the immediate post-Tiananmen period. The economic sanctions, including the export control and technology transfer provisions, are measured and appropriate. The President's veto of the Chinese student bill was also measured and appropriate. His success was based not only on the merits of the narrow issue involved but also on the favorable results of his overall diplomacy toward the crumbling Soviet bloc, particularly in both conventional and strategic arms control talks with the USSR. Whatever the results of the President's policy toward China, one fundamental alteration in our bilateral relationship must occur: the elevation of human rights to a core element of the U.S.-China diplomatic agenda.

Forty years ago the United States put human rights on the U.S.-Soviet bilateral agenda. Few believed that the inclusion of human rights on the agenda of such a repressive regime would work, but the events of the past few years show the strategy's success. The Soviet Union, as we have seen, has improved its human rights record. Perhaps at this point, it is appropriate to take the same approach to China. The Congress must insist that human rights be inserted in any prospective talks with Beijing. I do not hold out the hope that the Chinese will change their behavior soon, though perhaps not in my lifetime. But it is time to face squarely what we have turned our back on for too long.

Notes

1. Admiral Crowe's remark appears in the *Christian Science Monitor*, September, 18, 1990, Section: The World; p. 3.

2. Mikhail Gorbachev, *Perestroika: New Thinking for Our Country and the World*, updated Perennial Library Paperback edition (New York: Harper & Row, 1988), p. 219. Unless otherwise indicated, all references to *Perestroika* are from this edition.

3. Ibid., p. 17.

4. Ibid., pp. 21-22.

5. Reference in Dan Oberdorfer, "United States: Events Take Bush, Aides by Surprise," *Washington Post*, November 12, 1989, pp. A23, A28.

6. *Pittsburgh Press*, November 3, 1989, p. 12

7. David Remnick, "Lithuania's Party Breaks with Moscow," *Washington Post*, December 21, 1989, p. A47.

8. David Remnick, "Gorbachev Assails Secession Moves by Soviet Republics," *Washington Post*, December 24, 1989, p. A21.

9. Ibid.

10. See Michael Dobbs, "Gorbachev Calls for More Rapid Change," *Washington Post*, November 22, 1989, p. A18, and William Drozdiak, "Soviets Offer Assurances on Germany," *Washington Post*, November 16,

1989, p. A41.

11. Blaine Harden, "Strong Soviet Influence Suspected in Sudden Departure of Bulgarian Leader," *Washington Post*, November 12, 1989, p. A23.

12. John W. Kiser III, "Soviet Science: Moscow's Red-Hot New Technologies," *Washington Post*, March 12, 1989, p. D3.

13. Ibid.

14. Ibid.

15. Ibid.

16. John W. Kiser III, "The King of Soviet Entrepreneurs," *Washington Post*, November 12, 1989, p. D2.

17. Ibid.

18. National Research Council, *Global Trends in Computer Technology and Their Impact on Export Control* (Washington, D.C.: National Academy Press, 1988), p. 187.

19. Ibid., pp. 192-195.

20. Ibid., p. 205.

21. In 1983 there was a flurry of attempted diversions of highly sophisticated VAX computers by Western businesses to the Soviet Union. Several of the export licenses for the shipments were approved by Commerce "apparently without careful consideration of the particular export circumstances and the militarily critical technology represented by the computers" (Steven D. Overly, "Regulation of Critical Technologies Under the Export Administration Act of 1979 and the Proposed Export Administration Amendments of 1983: American Business versus National Security," *North Carolina Journal of International Law and Commercial Regulation* 10, 2 [Spring 1985], p. 447). In all likelihood, one or more shipments of VAXs made it to the Soviet Union, providing it with the basis for producing clones.

22. Joel M. Snyder, "Pact Countries Clone U.S. Computers," *Technology Security* (December 1988), pp. 10-14.

23. Ibid., p. 12.

24. National Research Council, *Global Trends*, p. 213.

25. Ibid., pp. 209-211.

26. John Burgess, "Link Sought for Soviets; 12,000 Mile Cable Would Complete Loop," *Washington Post*, November 17, 1989, p. C13.

27. Gorbachev, *Perestroika*, p. 181.

28. Richard Morin, "58% Say Cold War Is Ending, 45% Back Arms Cuts, Poll Finds," *Washington Post*, November 23, 1989, p. A22

29. Paula Stern, "Don't Oversell Soviet Trade," *Washington Post*, July 30, 1989, p. C2.

30. Gorbachev, *Perestroika*, p. 209.

31. Today Show, November 16, 1989, and *Washington Post*, November 17,

1989.

32. This section relies heavily on Homer E. Moyer, Jr., and Linda A. Mabry, *Export Controls as Instruments of Foreign Policy* (Washington, D.C.: International Law Institute,1985), esp. pp. 26-58, and Vladimir N. Pregelj, *U.S. Foreign Trade Sanctions Imposed for Foreign Policy Reasons in Force as of April 10, 1988,* Congressional Research Service (Washington, D.C.: Library of Congress, 1988).

33. David Ignatius, "While Washington Slept...; An Empire Is Crumbling, and the Germans Are Getting All the Goodies," *Washington Post,* November 19, 1989, p. D2.

34. "U.S. Equipment May Help Arm Soviets," *Washington Times,* January 18, 1989, p. A1.

35. Ibid. Quotes are by Frank Gaffney, president of the Center for Security Policy, criticizing the joint venture.

36. "Alcatel's Soviet Joint Venture," (Washington, D.C.: Center for Security Policy, March 21, 1989); "Britain to Defy U.S. in High-Tech Export to Soviets," *Washington Times,* April 27, 1989, p. A3; "Allies Defy U.S. on High-Tech Sales to Soviets," *Wall Street Journal,* May 3, 1989, Sect. 2, p. 8; "U.S. Sells Know-How for Arms to Soviets," *Washington Times,* January 19, 1989,p. A1; and, "Beware of High-Tech Exports," editorial, *Washington Times,* January 31, 1989, p. F2.

37. "U.S., Soviets Team Up to Announce Their First Joint U.N. Resolution," *Washington Post,* November 4, 1989, p. A18.

38. *East-West Trade Trends,* Fourth Battle Act, second half of 1953, p. 37.

39. "Bush's List of Proposals to Improve U.S.-Soviet Relations," *Washington Post,* December 6, 1989, p. A25.

40. U.S. Department of Defense, *Soviet Military Power: Prospects for Change, 1989* (Washington, D.C.: U.S. Government Printing Office, 1989) p. 140.

41. "Despite Speeches, Quayle and Baker Agree on Soviets, Aides Say," *Washington Post,* October 19, 1989, p. A24.

42. "Soviets Maintain Communist Party in the Vanguard; East Europe's Pluralist Plans Find No Reasonance in Moscow," *Washington Post,* November 13, 1989, p. A21.

43. Ibid.

44. "East Germany Faces New Challenges; Porous Border May Force Economic Steps Avoided by Rest of Bloc", *Washington Post,* November 15, 1989, p. A1.

45. Quoted in ibid.

46. "Apocalyptic Critics Offer Scenarios for Collapse of Perestroika," *Washington Post,* November 4, 1989, p. A17.

47. See Holman Jenkins, Jr., "High Tech in State of Siege," *Insight* Vol. 5, 1, (January 2, 1989), p. 15.

48. Felix A. Rohatyn, "Who Pays for Eastern Europe?" *Washington Post,* August 20, 1989, p. B2.

49. *Congressional Record,* November 17, 1989, pp. H8942–H8943. My floor statement introducing the amendment before it went to conference appears in the *Congressional Record,* November 13, 1989, pp. S15442–S15443.

50. William Dawkins and David Goodhart, "Deciding When It's Safe to Sell," *London Financial Times,* November 2, 1989, p. 8.

51. Ibid. See also, Giovanni de Briganti, "U.S. Denies Dispute with COCOM Nations on East Bloc Exports," *Defense News,* October 30, 1989, p. 5, and Kenneth R. Timmerman, "It's Too Early to Relax Technology Curbs for East Bloc," *Wall Street Journal,* November 20, 1989, p. A19.

52. A. D. Horne, "Warsaw Pact Countries Agree Each Can Pace Own Reforms," *Washington Post,* July 9, 1989, p. A20.

53. Quoted in Ibid.

54. Mary Battiata, "Shevardnadze Suggests Warsaw Pact Changes," *Washington Post,* November 26, 1989, p. A43.

55. Ibid.

56. R. Jeffrey Smith, "Military Leaders of East and West Conferring as Europe Changes," *Washington Post,* January 16, 1990, p. A20.

57. Glenn Frankel, "East Bloc Spars Over Trade Pact," *Washington Post,* January 10, 1990, p. B1, and "Comecon Nations Agree on Market-Based Trade," *Washington Post,* January 11, 1990, p. B1.

58. Winston Lord, "China and America: Beyond the Big Chill," *Foreign Affairs,* 68, 4 (Fall 1989), p. 1.

59. Graeme Browning, "After Tiananmen, Ominous Signs on Road to China," *Washington Post,* November 5, 1989, p. H15.

60. Title 9, Foreign Relations Authorization Act, Fiscal Years 1990 and 1991 (H.R. 3792), *Congressional Record,* November 21, 1989, pp. H9271–H9294. The China Amendment is on pp. H9291–H9293.

61. According to the Department of Commmerce, the value of licenses approved does not reflect the value of actual licensed shipments, which is substantially less.

62. For industry attitudes toward the use of foreign policy controls against China see, the statement by the American Electronics Association and Electronic Industries Association before the House Foreign Affairs Committee, Subcommittees on International Economic Policy and Trade, Human Rights and Asian and Pacific Affairs, July 19, 1989, and the statement of Howard Lewis III, Vice President, International Economic Affairs, National Association of Manufacturers, on "Foreign Policy Controls Against China," before the same House Foreign Affairs Committee hearing, July 19, 1989.

63. Hoffman and Marcou, "Law and Society," *Washington Post,* November 5, 1989, p. C3.

64. Lord, "China and America," p. 2.

65. Daniel Southerland, "Bush Envoys Visit China to Improve Ties," *Washington Post*, December 10, 1989, p. A1.

66. Ibid.   See also, "The China Mission", p. A14 and "Explaining the China Mission," p. A24 in the *Washington Post*, December 11 and 12, 1989; A. M. Rosenthal, "Betrayal in Beijing," *New York Times*, December 12, 1989, p. A25 "Hailing the Butchers of Beijing," *New York Times*, December 12, 1989; p. A24 and "Indecent Interval," the *Wall Street Journal*, December 12, 1989, p. 20.

67. Ann Devroy and David Hoffman, "White House Reveals Earlier China Mission," *Washington Post*, December 19, 1989, p. A1.

68. Michael Weisskopf, "Baker Outlines Goals of Mission to Beijing," *Washington Post*, December 11, 1989, p. A25, and David Hoffman and Don Oberdorfer, "China Trip Defended by Bush," *Washington Post*, December 12, 1989, p. A1.

69. David Hoffman and Ann Devroy, "Bush Rejects New Sanctions for China, Clears Satellites," *Washington Post*, December 20, 1989, p. A1.

4

Economic Security Interests

The global marketplace is in the throes of a convulsive transition. The most significant development, from the United States' point of view, is that we no longer dominate the international marketplace. Since 1972 the United States net international investment position (NIIP) has fallen from a balance of $37 billion (with a high of $141 billion in 1982) to a negative $368 billion at the end of 1987. Net foreign debt, one of the many components of the NIIP, exceeds that of all the Latin American countries combined.

The United States has also lost its dominance in the high technology marketplace as defense and industrial industries diversify globally. The international marketplace, along with the geopolitical system, has become multipolar, with major economic and financial centers developing in Europe (the Economic Community of 1992, or EC-92) and Asia (Japan and the East Asian newly industrialized countries, or NICs). The repercussions of the changing nature of the international marketplace are global, but nowhere are they stronger than in the United States, and nowhere more obvious than in the 1988 Trade Bill.

The 1988 Omnibus Trade Bill

The 1988 Trade Bill engraved into the national consciousness two very important notions. First, EAA reforms demonstrated that national and economic security interests were fundamentally linked; and, second, the establishment of the Competitiveness Policy Council acknowledged the need to reverse the decline of U.S. industry and stem the further deterioration of U.S. defense industrial and technological bases.

Why such concerns? Foreign governments have adopted increasingly aggressive marketing strategies through a variety of well-coordinated and integrated economic policies--most notably subsidies for their export-oriented industries and protective measures against competitive imports--to erect officially sanctioned trade barriers that have impeded U.S. trade competitiveness. Trade barriers; the growing dependence on foreign sources of raw materials and critical manufactured goods, including high technology products; and reliance on foreign investment and foreign researchers in U.S. institutions of higher education have converged domestically to coin a new concept of international relations, "economic security." Economic security as an operational concept may be defined, for the purpose of this book, as the recognition of the growing interdependence of economic, defense, and foreign policies and the need to preserve, strengthen, and coordinate the vital sectors of the U.S. economy that constitute the defense industrial and technology base.

Defense Industrial and Technology Base

Four recent assessments of the U.S. defense industrial and technology base project a grim picture of the ability of the U.S. economy to support a war effort under current conditions. The Air Force Association concluded that the United States and its allies are not prepared to sustain a conventional war much beyond thirty days and that U.S. industry today could not meet wartime mobilization requirements in less than eighteen months.[1]

The Defense Science Board, proclaiming that the "days of Fortress America are past," found that the continued deterioration of the U.S. industrial and technology base has diminished the credibility of our deterrent.[2] The Congressional Office of Technological Assessment, in its evaluation of the defense technology base, concluded:

> Technological superiority has been a cornerstone of United States security and industry since World War II. That cornerstone is not crumbling, but over the past decade it has weathered significantly. Foreign companies have made deep inroads into high-technology markets that had been more or less the exclusive domain of U.S. industry. In addition to causing economic problems, this has fostered dependence on foreign sources for defense equipment at a time when the technology in defense systems comes increasingly from the civilian sector. At the same time, the Department of Defense reports that Soviet defense technology is catching up with ours, and sophisticated Western technology is routinely sold to third world nations.[3]

The Center for Strategic and International Studies provided bleak figures to illustrate the decline of domestic sources of production. It found that in 1982 over 118,000 firms provided goods to DOD in 215 critical defense sectors, accounting for 90 percent of all DOD purchases. By 1987 the number had shrunk to only 38,000, a reduction of 80,000 suppliers. In addition, CSIS found that between 1982 and 1987 more than 4,000 firms left the airframe structural components industry, more than 600 firms left the antifriction bearings business, 890 of 1,310 firms no longer sold powered valves to DOD, and 668 of 834 businesses stopped supplying navigational instruments.[4]

These assessments generally blame this state of affairs on the decline of the U.S. defense budget, changes in the world economy, bureaucratic ineptitude and corruption in the defense procurement system, conflicts between dependence ("buy American") and interdependence (arms cooperation) policies, and long-term neglect of the health of the U.S. industrial base by both public and private sectors. Then, too, whereas foreign governments have adopted policies to ensure that their industries remain innovative and internationally competitive, the U.S. government has heretofore not systematically promoted such policies. Indeed, the relationship of the government to industry has often been, in the main, an adversarial one.

An Industrial Policy for the United States?

Unfortunately, there are signs that the current administration, like its predecessor, will pursue this same nonpolicy. It has apparently embarked on a course to cut Defense Department programs that bolster commercial research and development. First, in September 1989, the press reported that Secretary Mosbacher had been reprimanded by the White House for allegedly advocating an "industrial policy" for the United States, which would have led to government subsidies for certain ailing technology sectors.

Second, on the eve of the public release of a report by the National Advisory Committee on Semiconductors, the *New York Times* (November 16, 1989) reported that Deputy Defense Secretary Donald J. Atwood had sent an internal document to the director of the Defense Advanced Research Projects Agency (DARPA), the Department of Defense's conduit to the private sector for commercial research and development programs, suspending further funds for high definition television (HDTV) research. The *Times* story claimed that "one White House official" had said that the Director of the Office of Management and Budget (OMB), Richard Darman, "believed that the research programs [such as HDTV] are not as valuable as many high-technology supporters have argued and that the programs can have only a limited impact on America's industrial base. [Darman] argued that the technologies are better developed with funds from business and industry." This story prompted several of us in the Congress to write the President expressing bipartisan concern over the future of HDTV and other key technology research projects.[5] At the same time, I stated on the Senate floor:

> This effort to root out the last vestiges of Government support for HDTV... goes hand in hand with the apparently successful effort by the Office of Management and Budget and the Council of Economic Advisers to block any effort by the Commerce Department and Secretary Mosbacher to develop a strategy for this industry or even to acknowledge that it is important .... For some reason, there are people in this administration ... who are terrified of what we have come to call "the IP word"--industrial policy--that they are perfectly prepared to sell out America's technological future in favor of a misguided view of how the world trading system in fact works. . . . The irony is that this is not industrial policy.[6]

The U.S. government has failed to devise any substantive response to the highly successful industrial targeting strategies adopted by other nations. Even the most efficient and brilliantly managed U.S. companies cannot meaningfully survive against foreign competitors whose governments protect and support them.

SEMATECH: A Relatively Successful Industrial Base Case Study

The best-known, and perhaps the most controversial, initiative in the "industrial policy" debate is the U.S. government's decision to provide assistance to the nation's semiconductor industry, which in the mid-1980s was in dire straits. In the 1987 National Defense Authorization Act, the Congress found that it "is in the national economic and security interests of the United States for the Department of Defense to provide financial assistance" to the Semiconductor Manufacturing Technology (SEMATECH), a consortium of fourteen semiconducting industries in the United States.

Chips, the end product of semiconductor manufacturing process, are used in virtually all advanced weapons systems and computer systems. In a comparison of U.S. and Japanese semiconductor manufacturing quality in twenty-five semiconducting products in 1986, the results revealed that Japan had taken the lead in twelve, reached parity with the United States in eight others, and was cutting into the U.S. lead in the remaining five. Indeed, the U.S. companies' share of the domestic market had dropped from 89 percent in 1970 to 64 percent in 1987. The consortium was provided with an initial appropriation of $200 million, $100 million from government and the remainder from industry, to ensure that the United States would have a world-leading manufacturing capability with exclusively domestic content by 1993.

According to current SEMATECH officials, the organization "is alive and well and working."[7] In testimony November 8, 1989, before a subcommittee of the House Science, Space, and Technology Committee, SEMATECH officials nonetheless expressed concern with the state of the U.S. industrial base. SEMATECH reported progress in its technical goals but reminded the subcommittee that SEMATECH alone "is not sufficient to return America to world leadership in semiconductor manufacturing."[8]

U.S. Memories: A Case Study in Failure

In 1988, eleven leading U.S. electronics companies agreed to explore the idea of pooling their resources to manufacture dynamic random access memory chips (DRAMs), which most personal computers require to hold active data while the PC is in use. The exploratory idea was in response to the growth of the Japanese electronics industry, which controlled an estimated 80 percent of the $9.4 billion DRAM market. U.S. computer manufacturers complained that the supply of DRAMs was drying up and prices skyrocketing. The answer, U.S. industry concluded, was to ensure the continued supply of DRAMs by U.S. suppliers.

In June 1988, eleven U.S. electronics firms, including IBM, Digital Equipment Corporation, AT&T, Compaq Computer Corporation, NCR Corporation, Tandem Computers, Hewlett-Packard, and LSI Logic Corporation, drew up a plan to create "U.S. Memories," a consortium of the U.S. electronics industry. The original plan called for the companies to raise $1 billion from pledges totaling $500 million and by borrowing another $500 million. The idea was stillborn. In early January 1990 the representatives of the companies agreed to abandon the idea for a number of reasons. U.S. companies were accused of being "short-sighted" and "unwilling to back their words with actions."[9] Lack of government support was also cited.[10] A *New York Times* editorial summed up the collapse of the venture: "The industry tried to help itself and Washington paid no attention. Though an expression of concern might have helped U.S. Memories, the Bush Administration dismissed a recent blue-ribbon report warning the semiconductor industry is in trouble . . . the foundation of some critical industry is slowly crumbling."[11]

The Defense Production Act

The one vehicle currently at our disposal to take corrective action on the problems of the U.S. industrial base is the Defense Production Act of 1950 (DPA). The DPA provides the President with the authority to mobilize the nation's productive capacities for national defense during periods of national emergency. The DPA also allows the President to undertake projects to preserve and enhance the defense industrial and technological base during peacetime. The DPA has been reauthorized and amended a number of times, most recently in 1984. It expired in October 1990. Renewal legislation failed to pass the 101st Congress.

When the Senate Banking Committee considers renewal of the act in 1990, it will look closely at the set of amendments introduced by Senator Alan Dixon (D-IL), myself, and others (S. 1379) that would:

- boost incentives to produce critical materiel by establishing a revolving fund of up to $250 million and expanding the class of projects eligible to get purchase and loan guarantees, loans, and grants;
- protect joint ventures working to enhance the defense industrial base from antitrust laws, while allowing public access to some of the sanctioned consortias' deliberations and records and affording legal recourse for actual damages caused by a consortium's unauthorized behavior;
- improve integration of national security and economic policies, including those on tax and trade; and
- encourage investment in the defense industrial and technology base and discourage unfair foreign competition.

The first three hearings on the bill have attracted an impressive list of witnesses, many whom were former government officials speaking in favor of it.[12]

Foreign Direct Investment and
Acquisition of Defense-Related Industries

In 1988, foreign direct investment inflows totaled $65 billion, reflecting continued strong foreign interest in U.S. manufacturing, retail and

TABLE 4.1

Foreign Direct Investment Position of Selected Countries in the United States at Year's End, 1988 (in billions of U.S. dollars)

	All Ind.	Petro.	Mfg.	Trade	Banking	Finance	Ins.	Real Estate	Other
Total investments	328.9	34.7	121.4	64.9	17.5	2.1	20.3	31.9	36.0
UK	101.9	18.8	37.0	18.6	3.7	0.9	6.9	5.3	10.7
Japan	53.4	--	12.2	18.7	3.9	2.9	a	10.0	a
Netherlands	49.0	a	17.2	5.2	2.7	3.2	4.7	3.3	a
Canada	27.4	1.6	9.4	3.5	1.5	0.6	3.0	4.2	3.6
Germany	23.8	0.2	13.3	6.9	0.3	-0.6	1.8	1.1	1.0

[a]Suppressed by Department of Commerce to avoid disclosure of data of individual companies.

Source: James K. Jackson, *Foreign Direct Investment in the United States*, CRS Issue Brief. Library of Congress, updated September 29, 1989, p.13.

wholesale trade, and real estate. This marked a 61.3 percent rise over the $40.3 billion of the previous year. The United Kingdom accounted for the largest share of the increase ($21.5 billion, or 33 percent), followed by Japan ($14.2, or 22 percent), Canada ($10.4, 16 percent), Australia ($4.2, or 6 percent), France ($3.8, or 6 percent), the Netherlands ($1.9, or 3 percent), and others ($9, or 14 percent).

On a cumulative basis, foreign investment in the United States reached $328.9 billion in 1988. European firms, principally British, Dutch, and German, account for one-quarter of the total foreign direct investment. As Table 4.1 shows, European investments are concentrated in the manufacturing sector, whereas Japanese investments are concentrated in real estate.

Foreign direct investments in the United States have produced mixed reactions. U.S. policy welcomes foreign investments and is governed by the principles of national treatment, most-favored-nation status, and the protection of investor rights in accordance with international legal principles and multilateral conventions. This policy recognizes that total direct foreign investments, estimated around $1.2 trillion, or roughly 5 percent of the total financial assets of the United States, have had a net benefit on the U.S. economy in modernizing factories, increasing jobs and exports, bringing in new technology and management techniques, and (generally left unsaid) allowing us to avoid the full impact of the twin

TABLE 4.2
Foreign-Controlled Assets in U.S. Manufacturing at Year's End, 1987[a]

	Billions of Dollars	Percentage of U.S. Industry Assets
Total	275.7	12.9
Chemicals	75.6	30.9
Stone, clay, glass	12.4	25.8
Primary metals	15.8	20.1
Petroleum and coal	61.5	18.2
Printing and publishing	13.5	13.6
Electronics equipment	20.8	11.0
Food products	25.9	11.0
Paper	6.8	8.0
Transportation	15.5	5.6
Other	30.0	5.6

[a]Estimates based on incomplete 1987 data. The transportation figures are adjusted to include auto plants of Japanese firms classified under wholesale trade in the official data.

Source: J. P. Morgan, *World Financial Markets*, Issue 2, June 29, 1989, p. 3.

TABLE 4.3
Control of U.S. Industry at Year's End, 1986 (Percentage of Assets)

	Chemicals	Stone Glass	Primary Metals
Domestic	67.5	77.2	79.5
Foreign	32.5	22.8	20.5
UK	5.7	6.0	5.8
Canada	9.4	1.8	5.4
W Germany	4.8	1.4	1.5
Switzerland	2.6	2.0	1.4
France	1.2	8.6	0.7
Netherlands	2.1	0.7	0.2
Japan	0.3	0.2	3.5
Other	6.4	2.0	2.0

Source: J. P. Morgan, *World Financial Markets*, Issue 2, June 29, 1989, p. 3.

deficits.

Tables 4.2 and 4.3 provide additional data regarding foreign-controlled assets in U.S. manufacturing and foreign control of selected U.S. industries. Foreign control of U.S. defense-related industries is of special concern. Critics charge that foreign investment in and acquisition of U.S. defense-related firms go right to the heart of U.S. economic security concerns. These concerns found expression in the Exon-Florio provision of the 1988 trade bill, which grants the President the authority to suspend or prohibit any acquisition, merger, or takeover of a U.S. firm by or with a foreign person or enterprise if he determines that the investment will threaten U.S. national security.

This concern is not unfounded. From 1981 to 1986, foreign acquisitions rose from about thirty-five U.S. businesses to over 120. Of the latter number, 36 percent were in the electronics and telecommunications sectors; 20 percent in chemicals, pharmaceuticals, and biotechnology sectors; 16.2 percent in the computer sector; 13.3 percent in machine tool manufactures; and 10.9 percent in the precision instruments sector. Since 1983, 196 (15 percent) of all reported foreign acquisitions (a total of 1,286) have been defense-related firms.

U.S. industry is rightly concerned that foreign ownership of U.S. defense companies will compromise classified information, redirect vital investment away from U.S. defense needs, and make the United States dependent on foreign resources, including foreign researchers in U.S. higher education and research efforts. According to industry sources, in the past few years almost 40 percent of all graduate students of engineering in the United States were foreign-born.

The Committee on Foreign Investments in the United States

The one government agency with formal responsibility to review foreign investments in the United States is the Committee on Foreign Investments in the United States, an interagency group chaired by the Treasury Department and including State, Defense, Commerce, the U.S. Trade Representative (USTR), the Council of Economic Advisers, OMB, and Justice. Since CFIUS was established in 1981, it has reviewed 140 cases, approved 135 routinely within the thirty-day review period, and has referred only five to the President under the forty-five-day time limit for cases reviewed for national security reasons. Of the five, three were approved, one was approved with conditions, and in one the deal collapsed before a decision was made. The following is a scorecard of CFIUS's actions regarding the five cases:

1. approved the takeover by Heulls, a West German firm, of a Monsanto subsidiary that produces silicon wafers used in semiconductor production;
2. approved a merger between Westinghouse Electric Corporation and a Swiss electric engineering firm, Asea Brown Boveri (ABB);
3. approved the purchase by Matra S.A., a major French defense contractor, of Fairchild Industries space and defense electronics operations for $245 million (Matra is involved in satellites, electronics and tactical missiles as well as non-military activities

such as mass transit and telephone systems.);

4. approved with conditions the proposed takeover of General Ceramics, Inc. (GCI), of Haskell, New Jersey, by Tokuyama Soda, a Japanese-owned soda ash company (GCI manufactures certain ceramic detonators for nuclear warheads for the Department of Energy. Tokuyama Soda dropped the nuclear division, restructured its offer, and proceeded with the purchase with Presidential approval.);

5. reviewed without action the proposed sale of a subsidiary of Grumman to an Indian buyer. (The sale was dropped when it was found that India was ineligible for the purchase because of unspecified export control restrictions.)

Exon-Florio Provisions

The 1988 Omnibus Trade Bill approved the so-called Exon-Florio amendment, which extends the President's authority to review foreign investments (Title V, Subtitle A, Part II). According to this provision, the President "may take such action for such time as [the] president considers appropriate to suspend or prohibit any acquisition, merger, or takeover, of a person engaged in interstate commerce in the United States. . . with foreign persons so that such control will not threaten to impair the national security. The President has fifteen days in addition to the thirty days allotted for such investigations to make a determination.

In compiling the determination, the President may consider factors such as (1) domestic production needed for projected national defense requirements; (2) the capability and capacity of domestic industries to meet national defense requirements, including the availability of human resources, products, technology, and materials; and (3) the control of domestic industries and commercial activity by foreign citizens as it affects the capability and capacity of the United States to meet the requirements of national security.

Whither CFIUS?

There are some who see CFIUS as the ideal committee to oversee U.S. industrial policy, a view the Bush Administration would clearly oppose. CFIUS, under the circumstances, appears to be doing the best it can. If it lacks one thing, it is the need for greater certainty and greater clarity to the regulatory process. The legal community should know which transactions are or are not matters of national security. In the past, the idea of a "negative list" has been tossed about. The list would itemize those areas that are *not* a threat to national security (condos, golf courses, etc.). The idea has merit, but it is not difficult to foresee items that will ultimately fall between the proverbial cracks. In the meantime, CFIUS should be allowed some time to absorb and implement its new legislative requirements. It is difficult, if not impossible, to judge CFIUS's effectiveness on the basis of five cases.

Declining Exports

Not surprisingly, the U.S. export control system, which is arguably the most restrictive such system in the world, has attracted its share of the blame in the United States and abroad for the loss of U.S. dominance of strategic trade matters. The Office of Technology Assessment (OTA), for example, suggests that one option for improving the defense technology base is to establish a "central coordinating activity within the Administration to ensure that dual-use technology is exploited in the best interests of the nation as a whole."[13] OTA goes on to argue that the United States, "with its focus on the Soviet threat, has placed its industries at a potential disadvantage in world markets through measures such as restrictive export and technology-transfer policies."[14]

The data are compelling. In 1986 the United States registered its first trade deficit in high technology trade ($2.5 billion). Between 1978 and 1988, high technology exports accounted for an average of 28.2 percent of total U.S. exports with a low of 23.3 percent in 1979 and a high of 33.1 percent in 1987, the year of the record merchandise trade deficit. As Table 4.4 indicates, the most precipitous drop in the high tech trade surplus occurred between 1983 and 1984 when it decreased threefold ($18.7 billion to $6 billion). Since 1984, surplus has averaged $2.72 billion; before 1984, $21.6 billion. According to the defense industry, in the last five years, U.S. defense exports have dropped 53 percent, from $19.72 billion in FY-1983 to $9.264 billion in FY-87. The U.S. share of the world defense market has declined from approximately 43 percent in FY-83 to about 20 percent in FY-86.

U.S. military products, industry argues, are purchased by foreign countries for the technology they contain. Because the military strategy of the United States is based on technological superiority, government controls have been established to ensure that the technology contained in military products sold abroad will not be used to compromise U.S. national security.[15] The defense industry further argues that restrictive trade controls have led to an imbalance between arms cooperation and technology transfer policies, a failure to implement foreign availability

TABLE 4.4
U.S. High Tech[a] Exports and Imports, 1978-1988 (in billions of U.S. dollars)

	1978	1979	1980	1981	1982	1983	1984	1985	1986	1987	1988
Exports (FAS)											
World	34.9	43.6	54.8	60.3	58.1	60.1	65.5	68.4	72.6	84.0	104.2
Japan	2.3	3.3	4.0	4.9	4.8	5.6	6.1	6.6	7.5	8.5	10.9
EC-92	10.6	13.8	18.0	18.6	17.2	18.3	20.3	20.9	23.2	27.0	34.1
EANICs[b]	2.4	3.7	4.5	4.3	4.5	5.8	6.3	6.2	6.6	8.3	11.4
Imports (CIF)											
World	20.8	23.4	28.0	33.9	34.5	41.4	59.4	64.8	75.1	83.4	98.3
Japan	7.1	7.0	7.9	10.7	11.2	14.4	22.1	25.1	29.4	30.4	34.0
EC-92	4.7	5.4	6.9	7.5	7.1	7.6	10.8	13.1	15.3	16.2	18.5
EANICs	3.5	4.0	4.7	5.4	5.9	8.1	11.1	11.1	13.6	17.7	21.6
Balance											
World	14.1	20.0	26.8	26.5	23.6	18.7	6.1	3.6	-2.5	0.6	5.9
Japan	-4.8	-3.7	-3.9	-5.8	-6.4	-8.8	-16.0	-18.5	-21.9	-21.9	-23.1
EC-92	5.9	8.4	11.1	11.1	10.1	10.7	9.5	7.8	7.9	10.8	15.6
EANICs	-1.1	-0.3	-0.2	-1.1	-1.4	-2.3	-4.8	-4.9	-7.0	-9.4	-10.2

[a]See Table 3.7 for Commerce's definition of high technology products
[b]EANICs = East Asia newly industrialized countries (Taiwan, Singapore, Hong Kong, and South Korea

Source: Department of Commerce.

findings that would benefit U.S. industry, the adoption of extraterritorial and U.S. reexport control measures inimical to the multilateral export control system (the UK, for example, has passed legislation to block U.S. extraterritorial policies), and the deterioration of the relationship between the defense industry and the U.S. government.

The net effect of these, along with the Carter and Reagan Administration penchants for applying our policies extraterritorially, has given the United States the reputation of an unreliable exporter, a bane to U.S. industry but a boon to foreign commercial arms exporters eager to fill the vacuum created by our mistakes. According to the Arms Control and Disarmament Agency, about thirty non-Communist Third World countries are currently involved in arms sales. The equipment is low-end technology, but in the long term, the result will be greater proliferation of weapons technology and more competition for the United States. This competition, coupled with increased trade barriers constructed by friends and allies, will undoubtedly further constrict the global arms markets in the decade ahead.

Trade Barriers

EC-92

By 1992 the European Community's twelve member countries plan to remove all internal economic barriers and become a borderless trading bloc, creating a single market of over 323 million consumers. The European plan will allow for free movement of goods throughout the community and will abolish technical trade barriers, such as differing national product standards, purchasing policies, and export-import licensing requirements.

It is not yet clear how non-EC countries will fare in the single market, but the prevailing fear is that EC-92 has the potential to be the ultimate trade protectionist system. Given the interdependence of the U.S.-EC market, trade barriers of the magnitude possible by EC-92 pose a potentially serious threat to U.S. economic security interests.

In 1988 the EC had a gross domestic product (GDP) of $4,727 billion, compared to the U.S. total of $4,795 billion and Japan's $2,841 billion. The EC is the world's largest trading bloc, accounting for 16.5 percent of world trade. When trade among the member states is included, the EC accounted for 40 percent of total world trade, compared to 14 percent for the United States and 8 percent for Japan. Intra-EC trade (trade among EC countries) accounted for 58.4 percent of total EC trade.

The United States is the EC's single largest trading partner. In 1988 U.S.-EC bilateral trade totaled $161 billion. U.S. imports from the twelve member countries represented around 19 percent of total U.S. world imports ($85 billion); U.S. exports to the EC were 23.7 percent of U.S. world exports ($76 billion). The U.S. trade deficit with the EC ranked third behind Japan and the East Asian NICs. [16]

The United States fared better on high technology exports to the EC mainly on the strength of defense exports to NATO. Consequently, in 1988 the United States enjoyed a high tech trade surplus with the EC of $15.6 billion. The volume of high tech trade not related to NATO's defense requirements is expected to become a more serious concern if the export licensing paper trail vanishes in 1992.

As we shall see in Chapter 5, the enforcement of exports by COCOM member states is one of the issues the United States considers crucial to streamlining the control lists or to the establishment of "free license zones" among COCOM member states. The common internal market has the potential to be the most porous trade control system in the West. Because eleven of sixteen COCOM countries are members of the EC, the implications of EC-92 for U.S. high tech exports are significant. EC-92 will converge with EAA changes in the 1988 Trade Bill to cause serious enforcement problems for a multilateral export control system that already has an uneven record.

The elimination or reduction of certain licensing requirements to COCOM countries and the legislative creation of a "license-free zone" with COCOM members similar to the one the United States maintains with Canada constitute an open invitation to diversion. This development underscores the urgent need for the United States to fufill its commitment to streamline the control lists in return for improved enforcement efforts from COCOM member countries with weak export control systems.

The U.S. government's response to EC-92 has been mixed. On the positive side, USTR has appointed an interagency task force to study ten EC-92 issues. On the negative side, the strategic trade community has not organized itself as well. Although USTR has a well-defined role in general trade policy leadership, this crucial component is missing in strategic trade policy. The Department of Commerce, which one would expect to take the lead, has been given a supporting role in a working-level committee not headed by any of the principal line agencies responsible for technology transfer and export control policies.

Japan

Japan's trade balance with the United States accounted for 40 percent of the total U.S. merchandise trade deficit in 1988 and nearly 60 percent of the manufactures trade deficit. The United States has had a high tech trade deficit with Japan since 1978, reaching an all-time high of $23.1 billion in 1988.

The convergence of Japan's merchandise trade and high technology surpluses with the United States led to one of the most serious trade controversies between the two countries when the U.S. government announced that it was prepared to assist the government of Japan in developing a next-generation fighter plane utilizing U.S. leading aerospace technology.

The FSX as a Case Study. On July 31, 1989 President Bush vetoed S.J. Res. 113, expressing the sense of Congress that the President take certain measures to ensure that U.S. commercial and technological interests were served regarding the proposed codevelopment of the so-called Fighter Support Experimental (FSX) with the government of Japan.

Briefly, the United States and Japan agreed to a two-phase program to develop a next-generation fighter based on General Dynamics' F-16. In the development phase, the two governments planned to develop six FSX prototypes on a budget of $1.2 billion, of which Japan guaranteed the U.S. firm 40 percent, or $480 million. This amount would yield an annual reduction in the bilateral trade deficit of less than 1 percent.

The problem, however, was in the second phase. As *originally* structured, the FSX deal gave the United States *no guarantee* of a share in the far more lucrative *production* phase, estimated between $6 and $8 billion. After years of negotiations, the U.S.-Japanese memorandum of understanding was silent on the crucial part of the program. There was nothing to stop Japan from scrapping the FSX altogether, only to resume a similar project later without U.S. assistance. In the process, nothing in the agreement prevented Japan from keeping the technological knowledge acquired during the first phase for the paltry sum of about $500 million. When compared with the $7 billion (in 1989 dollars) General Dynamics invested to develop and produce the F-16, the prevalent view in the Congress was that the FSX was a steal for Japan. The administration only belatedly appears to have reached the same conclusion.

The agreement also lacked a stringent technology safeguard regime to protect U.S. sensitive technology from being compromised or even diverted. The Toshiba diversion still weighed heavily on the Congress. Finally, proponents of the FSX argued that the United States had to "keep its word" and go forward with the deal, flaws and all. Congress, as I wrote in the *Washington Post* (March 30, 1989), "was not a part of that commitment and had an obligation to review it."

With respect to that obligation, Senator John Danforth (R-MO) argued that the Constitution was clear in its assignment of the regulation of interstate and foreign commerce to the Congress. The entire basis of the President's authority to control exports, for example, rests on the statutory authority of the Export Administration Act and the Arms Export Control Act--authority explicitly granted him by the Congress. When the Export Administration Act expired for a few months in 1984 and 1985, the President was able to maintain our control structure only by declaring a national emergency--pursuant to other authority he was explicitly granted by Congress--the International Emergency Economic Powers Act. There was no question, then, that the basis for the President's authority in these areas proceeds from statutes enacted by the Congress. There was likewise no question that the constraints imposed on this deal by the Congress are well within the parameters of interstate and foreign commerce, as Senator Danforth made clear.

To support the President on this veto, therefore, was to deny to Congress constitutional authority it has exercised for two hundred years. Even though the override was lost by one vote, however, there was a sense of victory in the Senate. The administration, acting on the Senate's concerns with the financial and technological aspects of the agreement, reopened the negotiations and obtained additional clarifications and concessions that responded to the concerns that had been expressed.

Specifically, the government of Japan guaranteed the 40 percent in the first phase, and committed itself to "no more" than 40 percent in the second phase.

Implications of the FSX Case. Nevertheless, the concerns many of us have with the state of the U.S. industrial base, and the future direction of our defense industry remain. As submitted by the President, the FSX deal would have enhanced the country's near-term economic and military interests. But it is the long haul we need to worry about, especially in the Senate. The Senate's unique role, conferred by the longer terms senators serve, is to look further into the future, to spot the reefs and shoals ahead, and to set a course that avoids them. We have begun to lose the lead our nation enjoys in aerospace because of deals such as the FSX. My concern is that FSX-like agreements will contribute to the demise of the competitiveness of the U.S. aerospace industry globally. I predict that in ten to twenty years, the U.S. aerospace industry will join its sibling firms in electronics and telecommunications in appealing to the Congress for protection or financial support to keep it alive.

It would not have been asking both governments too much to sit down and negotiate a safeguard regime comparable to the U.S.-Japanese supercomputer safeguard regime. The latter not only specifies the design of the building housing the supercomputer but prevents certain buyers from even looking at the supercomputer machine, much less operating it. We should not treat our next-generation fighter technology with any less care.[17]

The East Asia Newly Industrializing Countries

Next to Japan, the East Asian NICs--Hong Kong, Singapore, South Korea, and Taiwan--together enjoy the largest trade surplus with the United States, $31 billion, or 23 percent of the total trade deficit. The United States has also had a high tech trade deficit with the East Asian NICs since 1978, reaching an all-time high of $10.2 billion (in 1988), second only to Japan's $23 billion.

South Korea, like Japan, has made a commitment to develop an aerospace industry by the turn of the century and sees the U.S. aerospace industry as its shortcut toward achieving this goal. And, as in the Japanese case, a proposed coproduction of a fighter plane, which was dubbed "the Son of FSX," attracted Congressional interest.

The U.S.-Korean Fighter Plane as a Case Study. In the late 1970s, the South Korean government committed itself to create an indigenous aerospace manufacturing industry. In the mid-1980s, the South Korean government approached the Department of Defense with a proposal to buy or coproduce 120 upgraded F-16s or F-18s (twelve purchased through the FMS program, thirty-six kits for co-assembly, and seventy-two aircraft licensed for coproduction in Korea). The Koreans narrowed their search to General Dynamics' F-16 and McDonnell-Douglas's F-18, ultimately selecting the F-18.

The South Korean government selected Samsung, the company that drove the United States out of the microwave oven market, to jumpstart Korea's indigenous aerospace industry. Korea had already gained invaluable experience building parts for the F-16 (e.g., the wet center fuselage section), doing piecework for the Boeing 747, and assembling the McDonnell-Douglas MD-500 and F-5.

The Department of Defense unsuccessfully urged the Koreans to buy a fighter off the shelf. The Koreans made it clear that the government intended to develop an indigenous aerospace industry and that anything short of fulfilling this commitment was nonnegotiable. Reminiscent of the FSX, our negotiators also caved in to Korean demands to develop a hands-on experience producing aircraft. Indeed, our negotiators concluded that "bending metal was not a problem for the Koreans."[18] All that was required to give the Korean aerospace industry its technology transfer capability was "management techniques and setting up an aircraft procurement system."[19]

The Problem of Offsets. Aerospace contracts commonly include provisions in the contracts called direct or indirect buy-backs or offsets. A direct offset is a requirement in a contract obligating the seller (the defense contractor) to transfer part of the production or assembly of the item (the fighter, in this case) to the purchasing country. An indirect offset requires the seller to market the purchasing country's products. Offset agreements can--and have--amounted to over 100 percent of the value of the item U.S. firms sell to another country.

In the KFP negotiations, DOD agreed to indirect buy-backs, a type of offset. This provision obligates the U.S. firm awarded the contract, estimated between $1.8 billion (according to DOD sources) and $3 billion (according to industry sources), to agree to offset that amount by purchasing a comparable total in Korean products, most likely spare parts for aircraft in the winning firm's inventory.

I strongly objected to the inclusion of the offset provision; I was pleased to learn that the Department of Defense also agreed. In August the acting director of the Defense Security Assistance Agency wrote a letter to the CEOs of General Dynamics and McDonnell-Douglas warning the companies that DOD would oppose the sale of U.S. fighter aircraft and technology if the winning contractor offered too generous an offset program in order to win the sale. DOD capped the maximum offset at 30 percent of the contract, in contrast to the 60 to 65 percent demanded by

South Korea.

Congressman John Kasich, (R-OH) in testimony before the Senate Banking Committee, spoke "to perhaps the worst aspect of offsets from the U.S. point of view":

> Offset and co-production requirements do not remain exclusively with prime contractors. Rather, the requirement for foreign licensing is levied by the prime contractor upon subcontractors who must then transfer a portion of their production, their weapon system technology, or both, to manufacturers in the purchasing country. To the extent that offsets result in an outflow of technology, the technology involved is that of subcontractors rather than the prime contractors who make the original foreign sale. It is therefore subcontractors who are ultimately placed at a competitive disadvantage from offset and co-production requirements.[20]

My second reservation involved precisely the transfer of technology to assist South Korea in developing an aerospace industry. Korean government officials publicly boasted that South Korea's goal was to have a competitive aerospace industry in ten years.[21] Whether this boast was realistic was not the issue; the issue was the stated intention to use KFP technological know-how as a springboard to develop an indigenous aerospace capability.

The Korean government has also said that the contract would be awarded to the firm that fulfilled both requirements. The *Wall Street Journal* (June 7, 1989) claimed that U.S. firms were competing "fiercely for the right to teach the Koreans how to compete with them." If the *Journal* was correct, I found the attitude of U.S. firms difficult to understand. South Korea may not yet be the kind of "technically capable foreign competitor" to arouse the concerns of the U.S. aerospace industry,[22] but this is precisely the same attitude of benign neglect that the United States took toward VCRs, TVs, semiconductors, microwave ovens, and automobiles. The aerospace industry is among the last of the high technology frontiers in which the United States has a commanding lead.

Clearly, neither our bilateral trade balance nor the competitive position of our aerospace industry could justify this deal and the offset connected to it. For these reasons, I introduced a resolution that called on the President not to sign any agreement with Korea until the General Accounting Office had time to (1) review the proposed deal for its impact on the U.S. industrial base and the U.S. aerospace industry, (2) assess the impact of the offset clause on the U.S. trade deficit with Korea and, (3) assess the implementation of Sections 824 and 825 of the 1989 Defense

Authorization Act regarding defense memoranda of understanding and DOD's offset policy. This key provision authorized the Department of Commerce to review Defense MOUs, a provision the Defense Department ignored during the formative period of the FSX negotiations.

Conclusion

U.S. national security comes in many hues and colors. Economic security is an important aspect of our national security. As a national security concept, it has only recently attracted the attention of the Congress, the U.S. government, industry, and the academic community. Export controls, as a component of economic security, have reached national attention as a result of the 1987 study by the National Academy of Sciences. Unfortunately, there has been very little follow-up to the NAS study, particularly the economic impact of export controls on U.S. national security. This book seeks to remedy that neglect by keeping the issue at the fore during the upcoming debate on the reauthorization of the Export Administration Act of 1979.

Notes

1. Air Force Association, *Lifeline in Danger* (Arlington, VA: Aerospace Education Foundation, September 1988) p. 1
2. Defense Science Board, "Report of the 1988 Defense Science Board Study on the Defense Industrial and Technology Base" (Department of Defense: Pentagon, October 1988), p. 1.
3. U.S. Congress, Office of Technology Assessment, *Holding the Edge: Maintaining the Defense Technology Base* (Washington, D.C.: U.S. Government Printing Office, 1989), p. iii.
4. Center for Strategic and International Studies, *Deterrence in Decay: The Future of the U.S. Defense Industrial Base* (Washington, DC: Center for Strategic and International Studies, 1989), p. 1 and 201
5. John Markoff, "Cuts Are Expected For U.S. Financing in High-Tech Area," *New York Times*, November 16, 1989, p. A1.
6. *Congressional Record*, November 19, 1989, pp. S16203-S16204.
7. *Update SEMATECH*, 1, 4 (November 1989), p. 1.
8. Ibid.
9. Evelyn Richards, "Firms Close the Book on U.S. Memories," *Washington Post*, January 16, 1990, pp. C1, C3.
10. "U.S. Memories: Too Short," editorial, *New York Times*, January 16, 1990.

11. Ibid.

12. The witnesses for the July 11, 1989, hearing were Frank C. Carlucci, vice-chairman of the Carlyle Group and former secretary of defense; Robert Costello of the Hudson Institute and former under secretary of defense; and Admiral Bobby R. Inman, chairman and CEO, Westmark Systems, and former deputy director of the CIA. The witnesses for the July 19 hearings included Robert W. Galvin, CEO for Motorola; Stanley C. Pace, chairman and CEO, General Dynamics Corporation; and Norman R. Augustine, chairman and CEO, Martin Marietta Corporation. The witnesses for the November 17 hearing included General John R. Guthrie (ret.), former Commander, U.S. Army Materiel Command; Lawrence J. Korb of the Brookings Institution and former assistant secretary of defense for installations and logistics; Costello; Albert W. Moore, president, the Association for Manufacturing Technology; Jefferson Z. Amacker, president and CEO, Leach Corporation; and Paul J. Gross, chairman, Proprietary Industries Association.

13. *Holding the Edge*, p. 115.

14. Ibid.

15. Electronics Industry Association Report, "The Global Defense Market in Perspective," October 11, 1988.

16. Glennon J. Harrison, Congressional Research Service, *European Community: 1992 Plan for Economic Integration*, (Washington, DC: Library of Congress, 1989), pp. 4-5. See also, Congressional Research Service, *EC-92 and the United States*, Library of Congress, 1989); *European Community: Issues Raised by 1992 Integration*, (Washington, D.C.: Library of Congress, 1989); and U.S. State Department, "GIST: The European Community" (November 1989), Office of Public Affairs.

17. On September 14, 1989, the day after the Senate had sustained the President's veto, Commerce Secretary Mosbacher is quoted as saying during a visit to Japan that "Japan will benefit more than the U.S. from technology swapped" under the FSX agreement and that "he was not completely satisfied" with the deal. ("Mosbacher says U.S. is getting raw deal on the FSX fighter," *Investor's Daily*, September 15, 1989, p. 4).

18. DOD briefing provided to my staff.

19. Ibid.

20. Testimony before the Senate Banking Committee on the Defense Production Act, November 17, 1989, p. 4.

21. *Wall Street Journal*, June 1, 1989, p. 26. See especially, "South Korea Drives Toward Greater Military Autonomy," in *Aviation Week & Space Technology* (June 12, 1989), pp. 176- 244, Vol. 130, 24.

22. Aerospace Research Center, "Facts and Perspective" (Washington, D.C.: Aerospace Industries Association, 1989), p. 1.

5

Issues for the 1990s

In James A. Baker III's initial visit to NATO in his capacity as secretary of state, he discovered what so many who are familiar with the arcana of export controls and technology transfer policy have known for a long time: The issues can be just as contentious as those in the sexier area of arms control.

The Bush Administration has been slow to formulate an export control policy. Indeed, during the reorganization of the National Security Council shortly after the inauguration, the administration decided to eliminate the position of special assistant to the President for national security affairs and senior director for technology affairs. The lone remaining staff member was a mid-level official who later departed the NSC. The incoming Bush White House staff did not include a senior official knowledgeable in technology transfer and export control policies to advise the NSC or the White House.

The agenda for the 1990s is already clear--and full. The Bush Administration, judging from Secretary Baker's experience in Europe, will find itself increasingly on the defensive and perhaps isolated from the allies if it is not prepared to address such potentially divisive issues as streamlining the control lists, implementing foreign availability provisions of the Export Administration Act, improving the export control provisions for chemical and biological weapons and the Missile Technology Control Regime.

COCOM

On July 6, 1989, Mikhail Gorbachev told the European Parliament in Strasbourg that COCOM should be "dismantled" to facilitate his notion of a "common European home."[1] In *Perestroika*, he says that COCOM is an instrument of U.S. foreign economic policy. Given such unilateral U.S. actions as maintaining the China Differential after COCOM abandoned it, the "no exceptions" policy, and more recently the use of COCOM to send messages to China's leaders for their arms sales policy, such a conclusion is understandable.

Recent Allied Views of COCOM

In 1990 the United States was is once again under fire for its conservative approach to changes in COCOM. The issue today is the relaxation of multilateral controls to the East bloc, specifically to Poland and Hungary. The West Germans believe COCOM is "outdated."[2] West Germany's foreign minister, Hans-Dietrich Genscher, reportedly told a radio audience in Bonn that Western nations "have to assist the reform-oriented countries [of Eastern Europe] via comprehensive cooperation and transfer of technology."[3] Italian President Cossiga, as we have seen, told President Bush on October 13, 1989, that the West should "review and reconsider" the restrictions on high tech sales to Poland, Hungary and other Soviet bloc countries.[4]

The consensus among government officials and industry leaders is that the only effective way to protect Western technological superiority is through a multilateral control system. Unilateral controls, as we have learned, do not work, and they can be costly. Yet rapid changes in Eastern Europe threaten to lead to breakdown of the consensus that created COCOM.

Streamlining the Control Lists

The COCOM International List (IL) is the heartbeat of COCOM. Today, it consists of three lists: the Industrial (or, dual-use) List, the Atomic Energy List, and the Munitions List (gone are the quantitative and surveillance lists). The International List is shorter than the U.S. lists mainly because the U.S. lists include unilaterally controlled items.

The COCOM Industrial List contains nine groups with item numbers that correspond exactly to the nine letter and number groupings and the export commodity control numbers (ECCN) in the U.S. CCL. The munitions lists for both COCOM and the United States remain separate. For the purposes of further comparison and illustration, a review of the COCOM IL shows that:

1. The COCOM IL has forty-one categories with administrative exception notes (AENs) and thirty-two categories with China green zones.
2. The CCL contains fifty-eight categories with advisory notes (AN, or the COCOM equivalent of AEN).
3. The CCL has nineteen categories with distribution license controls (important for implementing the DL to China).
4. The COCOM and U.S. Munitions Lists contain thirteen categories liberalized for favorable consideration treatment to China.
5. China is the only proscribed destination with liberalized export controls in both the dual-use and munitions lists.
6. The United States has never published the COCOM IL. The UK and Canada have. The 1988 Omnibus Trade Bill mandates the publication of the COCOM IL, but it has not occurred to date.

The first streamlining of the COCOM control lists occurred, as we have seen, in 1954. Thirty-six years later, it is by far the most controversial issue facing the United States and COCOM as we enter the new decade. COCOM's future effectiveness depends on its success or failure in resolving this issue. It is no exaggeration to say that the United States holds the key to that success or failure. Cossiga compared COCOM's control list and procedures to "dogma that is highly complicated and outdated."[5] The Italian foreign minister also argued that rapid technological change had made existing controls obsolete.[6]

In January 1988 COCOM held the first-ever Senior Political Meeting (SPM). The U.S. delegation was headed by Deputy Secretary John Whitehead, the highest-ranking U.S. government official ever to attend a COCOM meeting. At the SPM, the United States committed to reducing its control lists in return for improved enforcement efforts from COCOM members. To date, the United States has not vigorously pursued streamlining its lists, except in the perfunctory manner established by COCOM in the 1970s to review annually one fourth of the COCOM list.

In response to this inertia, the 1988 Omnibus Trade and Competitiveness Act mandated the elimination from the Commodity Control List of low-end technologies that are subject only to national discretion (or administrative exceptions notes). Equally important, the act mandated the elimination of unilaterally controlled items, except where there is no foreign availability or the United States is "actively" pursuing negotiations with other countries to control those goods multilaterally. These measures, however, amount to only minor changes in the lengthy and complex CCL.

One of the prevailing assumptions in the U.S. export community--made clear in the 1987 NAS study--is that there is no effective mechanism for weeding out from the control lists items that are no longer strategic or are readily available from non-COCOM sources. In fact, there is the potential for such mechanisms, but they have been blocked by interagency turf disputes. Consider, for example, the fate of one new and promising conceptual methodology developed jointly between a private consulting firm and the intelligence community:

CASTAR

Several years ago, the Futures Group, a research and consulting firm, cooperated in a government research project under the direction of the Technology Transfer Intelligence Committee (TTIC). This special project, initiated by the Director of Central Intelligence (DCI), was tasked with identifying currently available Western technologies that, if obtained by the Soviet Union, could aid it in the development of future weapons systems. The effort was entitled Project CASTAR (Center for Anticipating Soviet Technology Acquisition Requirements). In addition to projecting Soviet technology requirements, the methodology also had promise as a streamlining mechanism.

U.S. and COCOM control lists are based on mirror imaging: We assume that the Soviets will build a military system as we do and will require the same technologies that we do. Therefore, we need to control the technologies used to develop our military systems. Project CASTAR, however, was not interested in knowing the U.S. solution to a particular weapons system performance parameter. It focused on Soviet approaches.[7]

Soviet R & D style and production practices differ significantly from those of the West. CASTAR's goal was to identify the manufacturing and production technologies that the United States should control by specifically focusing on a subset of critical (or bottleneck) technologies *essential* to future weapons systems development. The assumption was that this approach would not only help to identify key bottleneck technologies but would also link those technologies to one or more future weapons systems. Thus, CASTAR had the potential for making a more sophisticated calculation of a technology's criticality, which, in turn, reinforced the justifications for export control.

CASTAR's methodology *as a streamlining tool* had also been applied to several test control categories in the CCL. The results were mixed. Some departments believed that it could serve as a streamlining tool; others disagreed. To be sure, some categories actually ended up containing more items to be controlled, others fewer. Industry itself had reservations about the approach.

Lost in the interagency dispute was CASTAR's potential beyond reducing or justifying the lists. CASTAR also held promise as an enforcement tool. For example, its proponents argued that manufacturers of the bottleneck technologies could be easier to identify and could be more easily alerted to the potential for illegal acquisition or diversion.

CASTAR was discontinued by a bitter interagency dispute questioning its effectiveness and utility. In late 1989 the decision was made to deny CASTAR the funds required to develop streamlining methodology.

CASTAR was originally one of two methodologies under development by the CIA's Technology Transfer Assessment Center (TTAC). Because of philosophical differences between the Defense Intelligence Agency and the CIA, DIA continued to develop CASTAR while the CIA developed its own methodology, which in time became known as Starbase (Soviet Technology Acquisition Requirements). Controversy and a lack of funds forced CASTAR to become integrated into Starbase. Starbase, however, has not fared any better. It has met with the same opposition as CASTAR did, and for the same reasons. According to industry sources, Starbase would have required an additional thirty to forty people and a budget increase of $20 million over five years. Starbase will continue its work, but at present levels of staffing and funding. In the meantime, whatever promise it holds as a streamlining methodology remains unknown.

The Critical and Emerging Technologies

The process of identifying militarily critical technologies is, nonetheless, well under way, even without the newer methodologies. The National Defense Authorization Act for FY-89 requires the Department of Defense to submit annually a Critical Technologies Plan that identifies critical and emerging technologies necessary to ensure the long-term superiority of U.S. weapons systems. The first plan, submitted to Congress on March 15, 1989, was sent back to DOD for additional information; on May 5 DOD resubmitted the plan.[8] In the plan, DOD identifies twenty-two critical and emerging technologies, excluding nuclear-related technologies. The plan argues that these technologies can only be effective if they are integrated into a balanced science and technology program with a full spectrum of mutually supportive technologies.[9] The critical technologies include microelectric circuits and their fabrication; preparation of gallium arsenide and other compound semiconductors; computer software production; parallel computer architectures; automatic target recognition; phased arrays; data fusion; signature control; computational fluid dynamics; air-breathing propulsion; high-power microwaves; pulsed power; hypervelocity projectiles; high-temperature, high-strength, lightweight composite materials; superconductivity; biotechnology materials and their processing; machine intelligence; simulation and modeling; integrated optics; fiber optics; sensitive radars; and passive sensors.

Enforcement as an Issue

Enforcement, as we have seen, has been on COCOM's agenda since its establishment. And since 1950, little or no progress has been made. COCOM, to be sure, does not have formal enforcement authority. Gentle persuasion, arm twisting, threats, demarches, or contentious bilateral negotiations remain COCOM's most effective means to prevent backsliding on this crucial component of the multilateral export control system.

Enforcement of multilaterally agreed export controls is and has always been the responsibility of the individual members of COCOM and is generally accomplished through national legislation. The result is a multilateral export control system with a series of uneven enforcement regimes. Indeed, some members of COCOM still do not have enabling legislation to establish an enforcement system acceptable by COCOM standards. It is within this context that U.S. insistence in linking streamlining to enforcement, a position that dates back to the early 1950s, must be viewed.

The Toshiba-Kongsberg Diversion[10]

The case that dramatically brought the issue of enforcement to the top of COCOM's agenda was the diversion of certain machine tools to the Soviet Union. In March 1987 the U.S. government learned of the illegal sale of eight propeller milling machines worth $28.2 million to the Soviet Union between 1983-1984. The United States believed officials of Toshiba Machine Company knew the sales violated Japanese and COCOM export control policies.

Specifically, the Norwegian firm Kongsberg and the Japanese firm Toshiba Machine, a subsidiary of Toshiba Corporation, had delivered the highly sophisticated automated machine tools to the Leningrad shipyard. In the case of four nine-axis machines, the numerical controllers necessary to operate the machines were supplied by Kongsberg Vaapenfabrikk of Norway, with Toshiba Machine providing the software and technical assistance to operate the machines. In the case of four five-axis machines, the numerical controllers and related software were supplied by Toshiba

Machine. To its credit, Toshiba did not provide the Soviet Union with a propeller design or with any U.S. technology. In any event, it is clear that Toshiba Machine deliberately deceived the Japanese Ministry of International Trade and Industry to obtain export approval. This was done by modifying the equipment prior to export, then restoring the equipment after installation in the Soviet Union to meet the Soviets' requirements, and by changing the model designations of the machines.

The machine tools, it was established, enabled the Soviet military to improve substantially their serial production of submarine propeller blades of approximately 10 meters (32.8 feet) in diameter, which, in operation, were approximately fifteen to twenty times quieter than earlier Soviet versions.

The threat to Western security was clear; less clear was the dollar cost required to offset the damage, although estimates were generally in the billions of dollars. One estimate argued that the diversion degraded the ability of the Western alliance to detect Soviet submarines by a factor of at least ten. This meant that for every one acoustic listening device that the allies had deployed to track Soviet submarines, another nine would now be required.

In response to the Toshiba-Kongsberg diversion, the Congress imposed retroactive sanctions on Toshiba Machine and Kongsberg. The companies were prohibited from exporting goods to the United States for a period of three years. They and their parent companies were prohibited from U.S. government contracting and procurement for three years. The Congress also authorized the President to impose similar sanctions for future violations of COCOM's export control regime.

Enforcement by Legislative Fiat

The Omnibus Trade Bill also amended the Export Administration Act by adding a series of measures clearly intended to strengthen the export control enforcement policies and structures of COCOM member countries. Specifically, the bill called for COCOM members to:

1. Enhance the public's understanding of COCOM's purpose and procedures by publishing the COCOM control lists;
2. Hold periodic high-level meetings;
3. Strengthen the legal basis for each government's export control system;
4. Harmonize export control documentation;
5. Improve procedures for coordinating and exchanging information concerning violations of multilaterally agreed export controls; and

6. Adopt more effective procedures for enforcing export control, including adequate training, resources, and authority for enforcement officers to investigate and prevent illegal exports.

Thus the trade bill linked enforcement with streamlining when it called on COCOM to improve enforcement and compliance with the agreement through elimination of unnecessary export controls and maintenance of an effective control list.

Rating COCOM's Enforcement Systems

Section 2415(a) of the 1988 Omnibus Trade Bill amended Section 5(b)(2)(C) of the EAA by mandating that three months after enactment (1) the Department of Commerce must submit to Congress a report that would determine which countries "are implementing an effective export control system consistent with principles agreed to in the Coordinating Committee," and (2) remove licensing requirements to any country determined to have such an effective control program. The House added the provision that countries whose export control systems were rated effective would become eligible for a license-free zone permitting U.S. exporters to ship many controlled products without a validated export license. The trade bill required Commerce to review and update the list of countries at least once a year, although countries could be added or removed at any time.

Legislative Criteria. The OTCA listed the standards the Congress believed were integral to an effective control system, mainly following principles previously agreed to by COCOM. The standards included:

*   national laws providing appropriate civil and criminal penalties and statutes of limitations sufficient to deter potential violations;
*   a program to evaluate export license applications that includes sufficient technical expertise to assess the licensing status of exports and ensure the reliability of end-users;
*   an enforcement mechanism that provides authority for trained enforcement officers to investigate and prevent illegal exports;
*   a system of export control documentation to verify the movement of goods and technology; and
*   procedures for the coordination and exchange of information concerning violations of the agreement of the Coordinating Committee.

On November 23, 1988, Commerce submitted its first annual report to the Congress but withheld judgment on the export control systems of the COCOM member states.   Commerce, with the concurrence of the the Department of State, argued that

> Prior to designating any country as having an effective export control system . . . we must consider not only the complexity of assessing a number of individual systems within our framework for measurement of effectiveness, but also the necessity of ensuring that multilateral cooperation for effective protection is not reduced. Moreover, we must take into account the important diplomatic aspects of the conclusions resulting from such assessment.[11]

Commerce revealed, however, that the requirements of the 1988 Omnibus Trade Bill "coincide[d] closely with the four elements agreed to in COCOM in the context of developing a common standard level of effective protection in the pre-licensing stage." These four categories included license requirements, documentation, review and screening, and national emphasis.

Based on the data collected for this review, Commerce "believe[d] the following to be true":

- Regarding license requirements, practices vary among the COCOM member governments concerning the publication of the control list, the availability to exporters of the procedures they must follow when applying for export licenses, the legal basis for export controls, and penalties for violations of export controls.
- Regarding documentation, practices vary in the requirements for import certificates, end-use statements and technical documentation in support of license applications depending on the final destination and the technology level of the products to be exported.
- Regarding review and screening, some countries appear to provide only a superficial review of applications for licenses to some destinations.
- Regarding national emphasis, practices differed widely in the level of technical expertise available to licensing authorities and their attendance at COCOM meetings.[13]

Unofficial Ratings. Where Commerce dared not tread, one Washington-based consulting firm did by undertaking to rate the enforcement systems for the COCOM member countries from data in public sources and interviews.[14]   The ratings are as follows (subheadings in the original):

The Stars	United Kingdom and France
Good Systems,	
Many Problems	West Germany
The Up-and-Comers	Japan, Spain, Norway
Small and Tough	Belgium, Netherlands, Luxembourg
The Goats	Greece, Italy, Turkey, Portugal, Denmark
And then there is	
Canada	Canada cooperates closely with the United States

These subjective rankings are not far off the mark. However, West Germany, Japan, and Norway have tightened their export enforcement systems considerably in the aftermath of highly contentious and well-publicized diversion cases. These three countries deserve to be ranked with the "stars" today. Spain is probably ranked too highly. It has enacted national legislation to implement an export control regime but has not yet published a control list. Spain's export control system is adequate. Denmark's export control system should also be ranked with the "up-and-comers," as it follows closely the practices of the Benelux countries. Australia, which joined COCOM in 1989, is an up-and-comer with star quality. Canada is a star as well. With the exception of Denmark, the "goats" deserve their ranking. Italy has an export control system without national legislation to back it up. Turkey, Portugal, and Greece rationalize the lack of an export control system with a lack of high technology trade or indigenous high tech base.

The Future of Enforcement

The U.S. government and COCOM explicitly committed themselves to streamlining and improving enforcement efforts during the January 1988, Senior Political Meeting. The commitment was reaffirmed during the October 1989 High-Level Meeting. Nearly eighteen months have passed since the SPM, and little progress has been made on these two key issues, which, in the final analysis, may become COCOM's Achilles' heel. In the meantime, Commerce (and State) will submit yet another annual report not in compliance with the 1988 Trade Bill. COCOM is currently reviewing the second part of its common standard exercise: postshipment checks, the enforcement part of the program. This part is scheduled to be completed by the end of 1991, at which time the entire program will bump up against EC-92. The implications have not been addressed, but as we have seen in Chapter 4, there will be some serious problems arising from EC-92 and the lack of advance planning on the part of the U.S. government.

In October 1989 the Italian firm Olivetti was alleged to have diverted sophisticated computer-driven machine tools worth $25 million to a Soviet aeronautics factory to help build the Yak 41, a vertical-takeoff supersonic fighter-bomber. Administration sources are cited as saying that the alleged diversion was potentially more serious than the Toshiba diversion case. Citing U.S. officials, the *Wall Street Journal* (November 10, 1989) reported that since 1983, European COCOM countries and Japan had delivered 6,000 COCOM-embargoed machine tools to the Soviet Union, and nearly all of them had been funneled directly to projects run by the Soviet Military Industrial Commission. Half of the 6,000 machines were obtained from West Germany. Japan, Italy, and Britain were also accused of violating COCOM's control list.[15]

Foreign Availability

Beginning in 1977, the Congress directed that products be removed from the control list if they were freely available to proscribed countries from non-COCOM countries, unless the President determined that the national security justified continued controls, notwithstanding the foreign availability. The 1979 EAA authorized the establishment of an office for foreign availability.

In 1983 the foreign availability program was begun as a division of Commerce, and the 1985 amendments to the EAA formally established the Office of Foreign Availability (OFA). The 1988 Trade Bill expanded OFA's responsibilities to include the creation of West-West foreign availability assessments, the imposition of new publication requirements and deadlines, an expedited licensing procedure in which eligibility depends upon foreign availability, and removal of controls on less sophisticated goods and technologies.

According to OFA's 1988-1989 annual report to the Congress, since 1983 OFA has completed eighty-three foreign availability assessments and reviews. Thirty-four of these studies dealt with possible decontrol actions; eleven dealt with new or ongoing foreign policy controls; three supported licensing decisions; twenty-seven supported the COCOM list review process that evaluates and adjusts multilateral export controls; and eight reports assessed foreign availability for new and revised national security controls.

In 1987 four assessments were forwarded to President Reagan for a decision on invoking a national security override: 8/16-bit microcomputers, jig grinders, wire bonders and sputter deposition equipment. The President decided to decontrol the microcomputers, jig grinders and wire bonders but invoked a national security override on sputters. Following the provisions of Section 5(f) of the EAA, the President directed negotiations with the source country. The negotiating period expired in September 1988 without resolution of the case. Subsequently, on June 6, 1989, the Commerce Department decontrolled some sputtering equipment and continued unilateral controls on other equipment.

The decision on wire bonders, however, was also not carried out according to Section 5(f). This is a classic case study of the difficulty of using foreign availability assessments as a means of easing the burden on U.S. exporters of products freely available to the bloc from non-COCOM sources.

Case Study 1: Wire Bonders[16]

On December 23, 1987, the Department of Commerce published in the *Federal Register* the President's decision to decontrol wire bonders West-West. In July 1988 Commerce circulated an interagency cable for clearance to notify COCOM of the decision to decontrol wire bonders West-East, thereby fully implementing the President's decision. The Department of Defense, however, refused to clear the cable and held up the decision in the process. Among other allegations, Defense asserted that Commerce's finding was based on faulty and incomplete information.

The case was referred to the NSC for a decision. After several interagency meetings, and with the probability that the Secretary of Defense would appeal to the President directly to kill the cable, the NSC opted instead to recommend to the President that the United States contact the government of the foreign producer to try to negotiate away the source of foreign availability. On July 17 the President authorized the State Department to make a demarche to the source country. On September 12, while the United States was concluding those negotiations, the source country promised, but failed to deliver on several occasions, a decision on whether or not it was willing to control the machines to the bloc.

What are the lessons learned in this case study? First, the Reagan Administration circumvented the EAA by authorizing negotiations after the President had decided against a national security override to maintain controls on the machines. Negotiations were appropriate for sputters but not for wire bonders. In the case of wire bonders, the President did not override the decision on the basis of national security.

Second, Congress provided for decontrol of products where there was foreign availability because such controls placed U.S. industry at a competitive disadvantage against foreign firms that are not constrained by export control policies. There is evidence that the foreign source country continued selling wire bonders to the bloc even as negotiations were in progress.

Third, lack of cooperation between Commerce and Defense led to the interagency gridlock that prevented a Presidential decision from being carried out. One of the principal findings of a February 1988 GAO evaluation of the foreign availability program singled out the lack of information sharing between Defense and Commerce as a reason for other foreign availability assessments' not being carried out. [17]

Fourth, the United States has led an initiative in COCOM to obtain cooperation from third countries in controlling exports to the bloc in return for liberalized licensing benefits under Section 5(k) of the EAA. Countries accorded 5(k) benefits agree to control technologies at the same levels controlled by COCOM. The United States has signed over a half dozen such agreements in the past three years, including one with the source country for wire bonders. Indeed, the source country is the sole nation to enjoy the full range of licensing benefits possible under 5(k).

According to the GAO report, one of the Department of Defense's arguments for blocking the President's decision was to focus attention on Defense's position that "once the U.S. government has granted a third country 5(k) benefits, that country cannot be considered a source of foreign availability."[18] This issue and this case, in all of its manifestations, has not been resolved. This has prompted a complaint from U.S. wire bonder manufacturers and a letter from the Senate Subcommittee on International Finance and Monetary Policy to the President seeking a resolution of the case.

Finally, this case revealed the availability of wire bonders in the bloc itself. Although the interagency meetings did not resolve the question of whether the machines met the standards of quality and quantity in determining foreign availability, U.S. industry sources claim that wire bonders manufactured in the Soviet Union and East Germany are as sophisticated as those produced in the West. If those sources are correct, it would strengthen the National Academy of Science's finding that technology trends today in computers and semiconducting equipment are toward globalization, commoditization, and foreign availability from non-COCOM sources.[19]

Case Study 2: Decontrol of Personal Computers

In the summer 1989 the U.S. public was treated to a classic bureaucratic war of words played out in the press between the Departments of Commerce and Defense. The conflict was over Secretary Mosbacher's decision, published in the *Federal Register*, July 18, 1989, to remove export control restrictions on AT-compatible and similar desktop personal computers[20] that the Department of Commerce had determined were available on the foreign market. Secretary Mosbacher's decision effectively decontrolled these computers West-West. Unfortunately, the media gave the impression that the Secretary's decision included the decontrol of the computers West-East. This was not the case. The United States was at the time negotiating that decontrol with COCOM, a prelude to total decontrol.

The Department of Defense made things worse by publicly criticizing Secretary Mosbacher's decision. DOD participated in the decision, and five working days before Secretary Mosbacher made the announcement, a letter was hand-delivered to DOD allowing DOD five days to register its dissent directly to the President if it so chose. Instead of taking its case to the President, DOD took its case to the public. Subsequently, the case found its way to the Senate floor, where one member called for a sixty-day suspension of Secretary Mosbacher's decision until the completion of still another interagency review of the issue.

The facts of the case make it clear that Secretary Mosbacher's decision followed the foreign availability provisions of the Export Administration Act. In an unclassified "coordination draft" of the Department of Defense's Militarily Critical Technologies List, dated June 23, 1989, the Department of Defense had reached its own conclusion that "computers performing technical and commercial applications that have PDRs of 100 or greater" did not have "intrinsic military utility."[21] The PDR of the computers that were decontrolled was considerably lower--68.

What are the lessons learned from this case study? The amendment to delay the decision introduced in the Senate failed to distinguish among the technical finding, the foreign availability determination process, and, more importantly, the politics behind the decision. First, regarding the technical finding that led Secretary Mosbacher to approve the Department of Commerce's foreign availability determination to decontrol the personal computers, the Department of Defense clearly established in the MCTL that the personal computers in question *had no critical military value.*

Second, regarding the foreign availability determination process, no one could argue that Defense was left out of the process. The Department of Commerce's AT Assessment Chronology clearly showed that DOD was included in the assessment from the beginning, January 27, 1988. On May 23, 1989, Secretary Mosbacher's decision was hand-delivered to Secretary Richard Cheney for his response. Between May 23 and July 13, when DOC informed DOD of the decision to proceed with the decontrol of the personal computers, DOD was in the loop at all times. From the beginning, Commerce provided Defense with the evidence to support its determination. In the end, DOD's refusal to agree with the decision to decontrol personal computers to the Soviet bloc had more to do with the politics behind the decision than with the technical finding or the process. In short, the Department of Defense, wrongly or not, based its decision on its long-standing position to deny the Soviet bloc *any* technology, whether strategic or nonstrategic.

This was not the first time that DOD has disagreed with a foreign availability finding for political reasons. Indeed, in late 1987 DOD challenged one of Commerce's first determinations, which led to a major evaluation of this decision by the comptroller general. The GAO found that Commerce had taken too long in making its determination, urged closer cooperation with DOD, and recommended that future decisions, including the evidence in support of those decisions, be published in the *Federal Register*. The GAO, however, found that Commerce had made the best decision possible given the information it had at the time.

Missile Proliferation

Since 1945, the Soviet Union has mainly formed the basis for U.S. national security concerns. In 1947 the National Security Act, an omnibus measure that totally restructured the U.S. national security apparatus, civilian and military (including intelligence), was enacted amidst the environment created by the Cold War. The act created, among other bodies, the Department of Defense, the National Security Council, and the Central Intelligence Agency.

With the advent of terrorism and terrorist-supported states, national security has taken on added meaning. Over a year ago, the current national security adviser, General Brent Scowcroft, co-authored a report that argued that U.S. armed forces may have to stop thinking only about Moscow and start thinking about the threat to U.S. national security interests from parts of the Third World. General Scowcroft was addressing missile proliferation but could have added the spread of chemical weapons.

Missile proliferation has reached a frightening stage in the last two years. According to a February 1989 Congressional Research Service (CRS) report, nearly twenty Third World countries are producing or developing the ability to produce missiles today. The possession of these missiles and the potential to arm them with nuclear, chemical, or biological warheads have added another destabilizing element to regional disputes in the Middle East, South Asia, and elsewhere and pose a new threat to U.S. and

Western national security in those areas. The CRS report states that "already some overseas U.S. forces are within range of the new missile forces . . . and future U.S. military operations in the Middle East, Africa, Asia, or South America may be hindered by the enemy missile forces."[22]

The Missile Technology Control Regime

On April 16, 1987, the Economic Seven (the United States, Canada, West Germany, France, Italy, Japan, and the United Kingdom), adopted the Missile Technology Control Regime to prevent the proliferation of missile technologies and related equipment. The adoption of the MTCR was something of a miracle in itself, coming after three years of intense and often acrimonious negotiations within the U.S. government as well as with the allies. Not surprisingly, the Seven could not agree on a formal arrangement and settled instead for an informal set of guidelines.

The purpose of the MTCR guidelines is to limit the risks of nuclear proliferation by controlling technology transfers that could contribute to nuclear weapons delivery systems other than manned aircraft. The MTCR commits the signatories to halt the export of technologies and equipment that could contribute to acquisition of missiles capable of carrying a 500-kilogram (1,105-pound) warhead 300 kilometers (186 miles). Because the items on the MTCR control list (the annex) span both the CCL and the USML, both Commerce and State have licensing jurisdiction for MTCR technologies and equipment.

The MTCR differs from other foreign policy controls in several respects. First, the MTCR is a multilaterally agreed set of principles. Second, the MTCR, unlike the COCOM control lists, does not single out a country or a set of countries as its target. The MTCR casts as wide a net as possible to prevent the export of missile technology and related equipment to all destinations outside the MTCR Seven.

Jurisdiction, Expansion, and Enforcement

The MTCR has created problems within the U.S. government, among the Seven, and with other major suppliers of missiles, missile technology, and equipment, such as the Soviet Union and China. The main problem within the U.S. government is jurisdiction over the MTCR. Commerce has licensing and foreign policy control responsibility over the MTCR; State has licensing responsibility as well as chairing the MTCR working group set up to resolve disputed cases, and, of course, is responsible for carrying out negotiations on issues related to the MTCR. Defense has responsibility for reviewing disputed licensing cases and fervently believes it should have complete jurisdiction over the MTCR; and ACDA and other arms control groups believe that certain provisions of the MTCR have the potential to undermine other arms control discussions and therefore believe the MTCR should come under the jurisdiction of the arms control community.

Within the Seven, the problems are just as serious. The main point of contention is expanding the MTCR's membership. The United States, for example, favors extending membership to the Soviet Union and China. Those opposed to expanding the membership argue that such countries will gain access to classified information on technology transfer programs within NATO. In any event, the Soviet Union and China have both rejected the MTCR, arguing that it is a Western condominium. The Soviet Union has shown an interest in negotiating a similar instrument either bilaterally with the United States or multilaterally with countries beyond the MTCR Seven.

Finally, the MTCR suffers from the same weakness as any other informal arrangement: enforceability. In hearings held before the Senate Armed Services Committee on May 3, 1989, experts testified that U.S. and Western European firms had exported controlled items to Iraq. Although the United States argued that U.S. firms had exported missile technologies before the MTCR came into effect in 1987, the export of missile technologies by Western European firms after the MTCR came into effect did not produce sanctions. The disclosures, however, have led some countries to adopt or tighten their export control laws to prevent future violations of the MTCR.

Chemical Weapons Proliferation[23]

The proliferation of chemical weapons has assumed center stage with the proliferation of missiles. The specter of missiles armed with chemical warheads, as was dramatically witnessed in the war between Iran and Iraq, has provided the United States with the impetus to develop an export control mechanism to stem this problem. According to U.S. government sources, an estimated twenty nations are currently stockpiling chemical weapons and agents. In 1963 the number was five.

As with the MTCR, the international community lacks an enforceable mechanism to curb the proliferation of chemical weapons. The Geneva Protocol of 1925 prohibits the use of chemical weapons, but it contains a number of loopholes. The protocol does not, for example, restrict research, development, production, testing, transfer, and stockpiling of chemical weapons. In addition, several of the signatories have amended the protocol either to preserve the right to retaliate if attacked with chemical weapons or to preserve political rights. Kuwait, Libya, and Syria, for example, have insisted on the right to withhold recognition from Israel.

Lack of Effective Western Export Controls

The proliferation of chemical weapons and agents adds another problem to the U.S. and Western export control system. Just as China's sales of CSS-2 intermediate-range ballistic missiles to Saudi Arabia in March 1988 triggered the strengthening and expansion of the MTCR, so the sale of chemical equipment and materials by two German firms to Libya provided the impetus to tighten export controls on chemical agents and precursors.

On February 9, 1990, the Director of Central Intelligence testified before a Senate subcommittee that U.S. laws were "probably not" adequate to prevent the export of equipment and chemicals needed to manufacture gases for chemical warfare. The DCI also revealed that firms in Western Europe, Japan, and the United States have helped Iraq, Syria, Libya, and Iran develop facilities capable of producing chemical weapons. Congress responded by introducing three bills in the Senate and one in the House. The bills all contain provisions for applying sanctions against companies and nations illegally exporting controlled chemicals agents or precursors.

U.S. Policy

In September 1989, President Bush delivered a major policy address to the UN General Assembly to announce a U.S. initiative to give additional impetus to concluding a worldwide ban of chemical weapons (CW). The President declared that the United States was prepared to destroy nearly all--98 percent--of its CW stockpile in the first eight years of a CW treaty, provided the Soviets joined the ban. Within two years of a treaty by CW-capable countries, the remaining stocks would be destroyed. The President also offered to eliminate, even prior to a global treaty, more than 80 percent of the U.S. CW stockpile if the Soviet Union joined in cutting its stockpile to an equal level.

At the September 1989 ministerial meeting in Wyoming, the United States and the Soviet Union signed an agreement that provides for a bilateral data exchange and verification experiment, to be implemented in two phases. Unfortunately, the initiative and the President's UN address were undercut by the U.S. announcement of plans to resume the production of binary CW weapons even while destroying all old, "unitary" CW stocks by 1997.

The Australia Group

Like missile proliferations, chemical weapons proliferation is a global problem. The solution, it would seem to follow, should therefore be multilateral. The Geneva Protocol does not appear to be the answer; indeed, one could argue it is part of the problem: The protocol allows the stockpiling of chemical weapons; it only outlaws their use.

The Conference on Disarmament and the United Nations have thus far been unable to forge an international consensus on an agreement to stem the proliferation of chemical weapons and agents. No one seriously expects an agreement to emerge from either of these fora until the next century. The only other multilateral organization with any potential to address the problem is the Australia Group, another informal consortium of twenty Western countries (mainly OECD, Japan, Australia, New Zealand, Switzerland). The group was established in 1985 in response to the use of chemical agents in the Iran-Iraq war. Its primary objective is to harmonize export controls of chemical agents, precursors, and equipment to all non-Australia Group destinations. Although the group has agreed to control forty-four agents and precursors, it lacks enforcement authority and its decisions are nonbinding. Like the MTCR, and to some extent COCOM, herein lies the problem with this well-intentioned organization.

To rectify this problem, I added an amendment to S. 195, the chemical weapons bill considered by the 101st Congress to urge the administration to strengthen the Australia Group by establishing:

1. a permanent secretariat;
2. a harmonized list of export control rules and regulations to prevent relative commercial advantage and disadvantage accruing to Australia Group members;
3. liaison officers to the secretariat from within the diplomatic missions to Canberra, the headquarters for the group;
4. a close working relationship between the group and industry, not unlike the September 1989 International Government-Industry Conference Against Chemical Weapons, held in Canberra, that brought together representatives from more than sixty-five governments and the world's major chemical manufacturers;
5. a public unclassified warning list of controlled chemical agents, precursors, and equipment;

6. information-exchange channels of suspected proliferants;
7. a denial list of firms and individuals who violate the group's export control provisions;
8. broader cooperation between Australia Group and other countries whose political commitment to stem the proliferation of chemical weapons is similar to that of the group; and
9. the imposition of stricter controls on the export of chemical agents, precursors, and equipment and tougher multilateral sanctions against firms and individuals who violate these controls or against countries that use chemical weapons.

The amendment has been well received by key members of the Australia Group, including some, but not all, departments of the U.S. government. Although the amendment is not intended to replace the negotiations under way in Geneva and the United Nations, it is more than an interim measure. Whatever positive results the Australia Group ultimately produces will almost certainly be carried over and adopted by the larger international organizations.

Notes

1. Kenneth R. Timmerman, "It's Too Early to Relax Technology Curbs for East Bloc," *Wall Street Journal*, November 20, 1989, p. A19.
2. Ibid.
3. Ibid.
4. Ibid., and Don Oberdorfer, "Italian President Urges Review of Export Restrictions; Cossigo Says West Should Reconsider Limits on High-Tech Sales to Poland, Hungary," *Washington Post*, October 13, 1989, p. A26.
5. "Review of Export Restrictions," *Washington Post*, October 13, 1989.
6. Ibid.
7. See, for example, "Soviet Requirements for Western Technology: A Forecasting Methodology" (Washington, D.C.: CIA, 1988), p. 3.
8. U.S. Department of Defense, *Critical Technologies Plan*, a report submitted to the Senate Committee on Armed Service (Washington D.C.: U.S. Government Printing Office, March 15, 1989, revised May 5, 1989.
9. Ibid.
10. Information based on Senator Heinz's office files.
11. [Review of the Effectiveness of Export Control Systems Pursuant to Section 5(b)(2)(C) of the Export Administration Act of 1979, as amended by Section 2415(a) of the Omnibus Trade & Competitiveness Act of 1988] Unpublished submission of the Department of Commerce to the U.S. Congress, November 23, 1988.

12. Ibid.

13. Ibid.

14. *Export Control Newsletter*, 2, 11 (December 22, 1988), pp. 3-7. Reproduced with permission of ECN.

15. Timmerman,"It's Too Early to Relax," and David B. Ottaway, "Olivetti Suspected in Technology Sale," *Washington Post*, October 12, 1989, p. 18.

16. Unless otherwise cited, information on wire bonders comes from Senator Heinz's office files.

17. U.S. General Accounting Office, *Export Controls: Commerce's Assessment of the Foreign Availability of Controlled Items Can Be More Effective* (Washington, D.C.: U.S. General Accounting Office, 1988)

18. Ibid., p. 40.

19. National Research Council, *Global Trends in Computer Technology and Their Impact on Export Control.* (Washington, D.C.: National Academy Press, 1988), chapters 2 and 3.

20. See, for example, Stuart Auerbach, "U.S. Relaxes Computer Sales Curbs," *Washington Post*, July 19, 1989, p. A1; Molly Moore and Ann Devroy, "Cheney Assails Relaxation of Computer Sales Controls," *ashington Post*, July 20, 1989, p. A10; Michael R. Gordon, "In Shift, U.S. Eases Computer Exports to Eastern Bloc," *New York Times*, July 19, 1989, p. 1, section 6.

21. Office files.

22. On November 19, 1989, I introduced S. 1924, the Missile Equipment and Technology Control Act, a bill to amend the Export Administration Act of 1979 to strengthen the efforts of the U.S. government to control exports of missile equipment and technology (*Congressional Record*, November 19, 1989, pp. S16224-S16227). For invaluable background information, see the Congressional Research Service, *Missile Proliferation: Survey of Emerging Missile Forces* (Washington, D.C.: Library of Congress, October 3, 1988, revised February 9, 1989).

23. Office files.

6

An Export Control System
for the 1990s

I do not believe that the U.S. national security export control system as it is currently constituted is prepared for the challenges of the 1990s that I have discussed in some detail in the previous chapters. For this reason, Senator Garn and I introduced S. 1796, the Export Administration Act of 1990."[1]

Although this bill constitutes a rewrite of the Export Administration Act of 1979, one of its specific purposes is to address the numerous problems I have mentioned through a sweeping reform of the entire process by which we control technology. The essence of the problems we have had for more than ten years has been interagency fratricide caused by inability to agree on either policy or process. The bottom line is a lack of leadership and discipline to the U.S. export control system.

Theoretically, a strong policy hand at the top could prevent the timeconsuming squabbles that have crippled the system. But the decisions in question are often ones of extreme detail, and it is unrealistic to expect the President--currently the only person at the top in a position to make these decisions--to occupy himself with minutiae. Indeed, both sides in the many struggles we have had over the years have learned this very well and know how to use referral to the President as a device to delay a decision rather than as a means of obtaining one. This bill would stop the President from being the chief licensing officer for the U.S. government.

This is the kind of tactic Senator Garn and I want to end, notwithstanding that we have disagreed in the past and will probably disagree in the future on the proper policy outcome of a variety of specific issues. For example, I supported the recent decision to decontrol certain computers, and I suspect he had some reservations about it. But we both had an identical interest in an effective policymaking process that can produce rapid, coherent decisions and that guarantees national security considerations will be fully taken into account. Delay and uncertainty do not serve the interests of anyone who wants good policy.

Such a process, unfortunately, does not exist at present. On the contrary, as I indicated, the trifurcated system creates incentives to delay or obstruct. It has led to endless debates about specific licenses and, increasingly, foreign availability. These are all arguments that should be made and addressed, but it should be done within a framework that guarantees a conclusion to the argument and a decision consistent with our overall policy goals.

The experience both Senator Garn and I have had for more than ten years is that such a process does not exist and cannot exist in an environment where control of the process is so diffuse. Our bill would streamline the system but in so doing would not eliminate the differences in perspective or even the fights between strongly held points of view. Instead, it would put them all in one office with one director and would thereby avoid the bureaucratic games that occur now. This would not prevent referral of important matters to the President, nor would it shut out the involvement of other agencies at the political level. It would, however, add unity, coherence, and efficiency to the process, which can only lead to better, more timely decisions. Our business community deserves nothing less, but they have had to live with much less for years, and it has hurt us grievously in overseas markets.

The second purpose of the bill is to refocus our understanding of technology policy in an integrated perspective that better reflects the role economics plays in national security. As the recent episode with the Japanese FSX program demonstrated, our government simply lacks the procedures necessary to take economic considerations into account in making such decisions. Had that deficiency not existed in that case, the entire embarrassing episode could have been avoided and some additional difficulties in our bilateral relationship forestalled.

The Office of Strategic Trade and Technology established by our bill would seek to gain that broader policy perspective through the creation of an associate director for economic security, whose responsibilities would include both the traditional EAA activity of short supply controls and administration of the Defense Production Act, Section 232 national security import relief cases, and monitoring of foreign investment. The OSTT director would have a seat on the Committee on Foreign Investment in the United States. These added responsibilities, along with the overall mandate of the position, would ensure that the administration takes an integrated approach to national security rather than the uncoordinated approach that is presently the rule. We should not have to have an FSX fiasco to persuade the government that perspectives beyond those of the Defense Department need to be involved in defining our security.

This bill is the product of extensive consultation with affected parties. In putting it together, we have discussed the contents of the bill with a number of industry organizations, including the Chamber of Commerce, the American Electronics Association, the Electronics Industries Association, the Aerospace Industry Association, the Business Roundtable, the Defense Policy Advisory Committee on Trade, Deltac, the National Association of Manufacturers, the Computer and Communications Industry Association and the Computer Business Equipment and Manufacturers' Association. The membership of these organizations includes a veritable who's who of those concerned with export controls and technology transfer. Obviously, not all these organizations or their individual member companies are in favor of this bill. Some oppose it because they are opposed to any change, some because they believe the bill creates a new regulatory agency that may become too powerful and work against their interests, and some because they fear that the efficiency and streamlining of the export control system will hurt their pocketbooks. Obtaining an export license is big business, and there are those who are making a good living from the gridlock and inefficiency of the current system.

Senator Garn and I, of course, believe that the bill is a good one, and one whose time has come. In our judgment the past ten years are dramatic testimony to the failure of incrementalism. We are recommending an entirely new approach, but we are more than prepared to debate this issue, a process that I hope will by itself facilitate an informed reauthorization of the EAA.

As outlined in the bill, the OSTT would have the following unique features:

First, it would bring under one administrative roof the control lists and the licensing systems established under the Export Administration Act and the Arms Export Control Act. Exporters would have one-stop license processing, and license referrals would be greatly reduced. For example, West-West licenses would no longer be referred to the Department of Defense, thus removing one major obstacle to their timely processing. The number of East-West licenses submitted for dispute resolution would also be reduced because of the centralization of the licensing process. Disputed licenses would have short turnaround times; days and weeks rather than months or even years.

Second, the bill would transfer the Bureau of Export Administration from Commerce, the Office of Munitions Control from State, and the

Defense Technology Security Administration from Defense to the OSTT. Although the bill would provide for substantive policy input from key line agencies, the OSTT would be designed to channel that input in an efficient and predictable manner missing from today's system.

Third, the OSTT would include three offices headed by associate directors, equivalent to under secretaries, for:

1. *Export Administration,* which would oversee the EAA and ITAR, including the control list, licensing system, technology policy, foreign affairs analysis, foreign availability determinations, and COCOM affairs;
2. *NonProliferation,* which would include foreign policy controls, such as chemical, biological, and missile nonproliferation; and
3. *Economic Security,* which would address industrial base, foreign investment, Defense Production Act, short supply, and antiboycott issues.

The Bureau of Economic Security is a new idea. It would function as an advisory group concerned with how national security considerations should influence economic policy and the decisionmaking process itself. I believe that if the current export control system had had such an office we could have avoided such difficult confrontations between the legislative and executive branches as the FSX and the Korean Fighter Program.

The notion of a Bureau of NonProliferation is also new, responding to the missile and chemical weapons proliferation, which has reached an acute stage in the last few years. About twenty Third World countries possess missiles with the potential to destabilize regional disputes and to pose a threat to U.S. and Western security. Many Third World countries with long-standing trade ties to the United States are among those developing missile and chemical weapons without accountability.

To counter missile proliferation, the United States and its economic summit partners developed the Missile Technology Control Regime to control the exports of missile technology and equipment. The MTCR, like COCOM, is an informal, nontreaty organization and therefore suffers from the same problems, particularly enforcement, as COCOM does. Further, the MTCR is perceived by nonadherents, the Soviet Union and China in particular, as a Western condominium that would relegate them to second-class status if they joined. Finally, the MTCR members cannot agree among themselves who should or should not join, or under what circumstances they should join.

The proliferation of chemical weapons has also become a threat to regional stability and to U.S. security interests, particularly in the Middle

East, where no fewer than six countries are seeking precursors, agents, and technology to construct chemical weapons facilities. CW use in the Iran-Iraq war, and subsequently by Iraq against the Kurds, has spawned interest in the use of export controls to deny materials and equipment for chemical weapons. One of the major missions of the OSTT would be to strengthen the Australia Group, another informal twenty-country group headed by Australia and the OECD countries to stem chemical weapons proliferation.

Fourth, the OSTT would provide for an Industry Advisory Committee (IAC) to ensure that the private sector has immediate access to the director. The IAC would have direct input to the COCOM list review process and its chair would be a member of U.S. delegations traveling to COCOM. We have never accorded our private-sector experts--the most directly concerned parties--the attention and opportunity for input that our trading partners have. Our businesses are not the enemy, and we should not treat them as if they were. The bill seeks to ensure that U.S. strategic trade policy is in approximate harmony to that of the trade-facilitating policies of allies and friends and seeks to ease the burden that export controls impose on U.S. manufacturers and exporters.

Finally, the OSTT would include a Strategic Trade Policy Council (STPC) made up of the secretaries of State, Defense, Commerce, and Treasury; the director of the CIA; and the U.S. Trade Representative. The STPC would approve export control and technology transfer policies, approve and streamline the U.S. unified control list, and resolve technology transfer issues arising from all bilateral defense, coproduction, and strategic trade agreements. The STPC would resolve only those licensing issues submitted to it by the director based on policy guidelines agreed to between the director and the STPC.

I see the interaction between the Policy Council and the director (who is appointed by the President, confirmed by the Senate, and has Cabinet-level status) as similar to that between the U.S. Trade Representative and the Trade Policy Committee or Economic Policy Council. The director would formulate export control and technology transfer policies subject to the approval of the STPC and would have the right to present the OSTT's position on cases directly to the President, as would the STPC.

The bill prescribes no increase in personnel. Initially, the cost of the operation of the OSTT is projected to be approximately that of the current system. In time, with the elimination of duplicative services and personnel, and the establishment of a single control list and one centralized licensing office, I foresee a reduction of costs and personnel. (I have asked the Congressional Budget Office to undertake a cost estimate of the system given my assumptions.)

I introduced this bill--and the restoration of this issue to the legislative front burner--with mixed feelings. In 1983 and 1984, I opposed Senator Garn's efforts to create a similar Office of Strategic Trade. Although the OSTT Bill is significantly different from that earlier bill, it is similar in that it acknowledges the failure of an incremental approach to EAA reform and recognizes that structural revision is an integral part of policy reform. Unlike Senator Garn's earlier effort,[2] this bill does not make major policy reforms--although it contains a good many changes to the EAA that are by no means technical. Instead, it seeks to confront head-on the interagency difficulties that have crippled the development of coherent policy over the years. I agree with Senator Garn that that is the proper place to begin.

I also particularly welcome the bill's acknowledgment that protection of our national security is conceptually a broader task than simply controlling exports of high technology goods. The OSTT's emphasis on the wider idea of economic security and nonproliferation is overdue, in my judgment, and will give the administration the structural tools it needs to formulate security policies that fully meet our needs heading into the next century. As I noted in the Preface, my role in developing the current export control system does not keep me from seeing that it is long overdue for reform. The OSTT Bill represents a step in this direction.

Notes

1. See the *Congressional Record*, October 25, 1989, pp. S14138-S14149.

2. See S. 434, The Office of Strategic Trade Act of 1983, *Congressional Record*, February 3, 1983, pp. S1011-S1032.

Acronyms and Abbreviations

ABB	Asea Brown Boveri
ACDA	Arms Control and Disarmament Agency
ACEP	Advisory Committee on Export Policy
AEC	Advisory Committee on Export Policy
AEN	administrative exception note
AID	Agency for International Development
AN	advisory note
AT	advisory note
BIT	bilateral investment treaty
BXA	Bureau of Export Administration
CASTAR	Center for Anticipating Soviet Technology Acquisition Requirements
CAVCTS	Combined Acceleration Vibration Climatic Test System
CCC	Customs Cooperation Council
CCL	Commodity Control List
CFIUS	Committee on Foreign Investments in the United States
CHINACOM	China Committee
CIA	Central Intelligence Agency
CMEA	Council for Mutual Economic Assistance
COCOM	Coordinating Committee for Multilateral Export Controls
CRS	Congressional Research Service
CSIS	Center for Strategic and International Studies
CW	chemical weapons
DARPA	Defense Advanced Research Projects Agency
DCI	Director of Central Intelligence
DIA	Defense Intelligence Agency
DOC	Department of Commerce
DOD	Department of Defense
DPA	Defense Production Act
DRAM	dynamic random access memory chip
DTSA	Defense Technology Security Administration
EAA	Export Administration Act

EARB	Export Administration Review Board
EC	European Community
ECA	Economic Cooperation Act
ECCN	export commodity control numbers
EDAC	Economic Defense Advisory Committee
FMS	foreign military sale
FSX	Fighter Support Experimental
FY	fiscal year
GAO	General Accounting Office
GATT	General Agreement on Tariffs and Trade
GCI	General Ceramics, Inc.
GDP	gross domestic product
GSP	Generalized System of Preferences
HDTV	high definition television
IAC	Industry Advisory Committee
IAEA	International Atomic Energy Agency
IC/DV	import certificate-delivery verification
IEEPA	International Emergency Economic Powers Act
IL	International List
IMF	International Monetary Fund
IML	International Munitions List
INF	Intermediate-Range Nuclear Forces
ITAR	International Traffic in Arms Regulations
JCCT	U.S.-China Joint Commission on Commerce and Trade
KFP	Korean Fighter Program
LOA	letter of agreement
MCTL	Militarily Critical Technologies List
MFLOPS	million floating point operations per second
MFN	most favored nation
MOU	memorandum of understanding
MTCR	Missile Technology Control Regime
NAS	National Academy of Sciences
NATO	North Atlantic Treaty Organization
NIC	newly industrializing country
NIIP	net international investment position
NNPA	Nuclear Non-Proliferation Act
NPT	Treaty on the Non-Proliferation of Nuclear Weapons
NRC	Nuclear Regulatory Commission
NRL	Nuclear Referral List
NSA	National Security Agency
ODM	Office of Defense Mobilization
OECD	Organization for Economic Cooperation and Development

OFA	Office of Foreign Availability
OFAC	Office of Foreign Assets Control
OMB	Office of Management and Budget
OMC	Office of Munitions Control
OPIC	Overseas Protection Insurance Corporation
OSTT	Office of Strategic Trade and Technology
OTA	Office of Technology and Assessment
OTCA	Omnibus Trade and Competitiveness Act
PDR	processing data rate
PEC	President's Export Council
PECSEA	President's Export Council Subcommittee on Export Administration
SCAP	Supreme Commander for the Alllied Powers
SEMATECH	Semiconductor Manufacturing Technology
SNEC	Subgroup on Nuclear Export Coordination
SPM	Senior Political Meeting
STA	strategic trade agreement
START	Strategic Arms Reduction Talks
STPC	Strategic Trade Policy Commission
TDP	Trade Development Program
TPP	theoretical peak performance
TTAC	Technology Transfer Assessment Center
TTIC	Technology Transfer Intelligence Committee
TWEA	Trading with the Enemy Act
UNFPA	United Nations Fund for Population Activities
UNRRA	United Nations Relief and Rehabilitation Administration
USML	U.S. Munitions List
USTR	U.S. Trade Representative
VOA	Voice of America
VPK	Soviet Military Industrial Commission

Selected Bibliography

Air Force Association. Science and Technology Committee. *The Future at Risk: The State of the US Science and Technology Program.* Arlington, V.A., September 1989.

Berman, Harold J., and John R. Garson. "United States Export Controls-- Past, Present, and Future," *Columbia Law Review,* 67, 5 (May 1967), pp. 791-890.

Bertsch, Gary K. (ed.) *Controlling East-West Trade and Technology Transfer.* Durham N.C.: Duke University Press, 1988.

Business Roundtable. "Recommendations for Improving the Export Control System." Unpublished paper, n.d. Cited with permission of Business Roundtable.

Center for Strategic and International Studies. *Deterrence in Decay: The Future of the U.S. Defense Industrial Base.* Washington, D.C., May 1989.

Center for Security Policy. "Alcatel's Soviet Joint Venture." March 21, 1989. Published by Center for Security Policy, Washington, D.C.

Export Control Newsletter. 2, 11 (December 22, 1988). Cited with permission of MK Technology Associates.

Gorbachev, Mikhail. *Perestroika: New Thinking for Our Country and the World.* New, updated Perennial Library paperback edition. New York: Harper & Row, 1988.

Metzger, Stanley D. *Law of International Trade: Documents and Readings.* Vol. 2, Washington, D.C.: Lerner Law Book Company, 1966.

Moyer, Homer E., and Linda A. Mabry. *Export Controls as Instruments of*

Foreign Policy. Washington, D.C.: International Law Institute, 1985.

National Academy of Sciences. *Balancing the National Interest: U.S. National Security Export Controls and Global Economic Competition.* Washington, D.C.: National Academy Press, 1987.

National Research Council. *Global Trends in Computer Technology and Their Impact on Export Control.* Washington, D.C.: National Academy Press, 1988.

Schwartz, Bernard L. *Foreign Ownership of U.S. Defense Companies: Where Do We Draw the Line?* Washington, D.C.: Johns Hopkins University Foreign Policy Institute, February 1989.

Schwartz, Jonathan B. "Controlling Nuclear Proliferation: Legal Strategies of the United States," *Law and Policy in International Business* 20, 1 (1988), pp. 1-61.

Smaldone, Joseph P. "U.S. Commercial Arms Exports: Policy, Process, and Patterns," in Louscher, David J. and Salomone, Michael D. (eds.), *Marketing Security Assistance* (Toronto: D. C. Heath and Co., 1987), pp. 185-204.

Spencer, Linda M. *American Assets: An Examination of Foreign Investment in the United States.* Washington, D.C.: Congressional Economic Leadership Institute, July 1988.

U.S. Congress. *Omnibus Trade and Competitiveness Act of 1988.* Public Law 100-418. Washington, D.C.: U.S. Government Printing Office, August 23, 1988.

U.S. Congress. Congressional Research Service. *Missile Proliferation: Survey of Emerging Missile Forces.* Washington, D.C.: Library of Congress, October 3, 1988, revised February 9, 1989.

U.S. Congress. Congressional Research Service. *Technological Advancement and U.S. Industrial Competitiveness.* Washington, D.C.: Library of Congress, October 28, 1988.

U.S. Congress. Office of Technology Assessment. *The Defense Technology Base: Introduction and Overview.* Washington, D.C.: U.S. Government Printing Office, March 1988.

U.S. Congress. Congressional Research Service. *U.S. Foreign Trade Sanctions Imposed for Foreign Policy Reasons in Force as of April 10, 1988.* Washington,

D.C.: Library of Congress, April 13, 1988.

U.S. Congress. Office of Technology Assessment. *Holding the Edge: Maintaining the Defense Technology Base.* 2 Vols. Washington, D.C.: U.S. Government Printing Office, April 1989.

U.S. Department of Commerce. *1989 Annual Foreign Policy Report to the Congress.* Washington, D.C.: U.S. Department of Commerce, February 1989.

U.S. Department of Commerce. *Report of the President's Export Council Subcommittee on Export Administration, 1985-1989.* 2 Vols. Washington, D.C.: U.S. Government Printing Office, September 1989.

U.S. Department of Commerce. *U.S. Trade in Transition: Maintaining the Gains.* A Report to the President from the President's Export Council. 2 Vols. Washington, D.C.: U.S. Government Printing Office, 1988.

U.S. Department of Defense. *Bolstering Defense Industrial Competitiveness.* Report to the Secretary of Defense by the Undersecretary of Defense (Acquisition). Washington, D.C.: Pentagon, July 1988.

U.S. Department of Defense. *Soviet Military Power: Prospects for Change, 1989.* Washington, D.C.: U.S. Government Printing Office, 1989.

U.S. Department of State. *Battle Act Reports to the Congress.* Nos. 1-26.

U.S. General Accounting Office. *Export Controls: Extent of DOD Influence on Licensing Decisions.* Washington, D.C.: U.S. Government Printing Office, 1989.

U.S. General Accounting Office. *Export Controls: Commerce's Assessment of the Foreign Availability of Controlled Items Can Be More Effective.* Washington, D.C.: U.S. General Accounting Office, February 1988.

U.S. General Accounting Office. *Industrial Base: Defense-Critical Industries.* Briefing Report to the Honorable John Heinz, U.S. Senate. Washington, D.C.: U.S. General Accounting Office, August 1988.

U.S. General Accounting Office. *Report by the General Accounting Office on Arms Export Licensing at the Department of State.* Washington, D.C.: U.S. General Accounting Office, September 11, 1987.

Index

ABB. *See* Asea Brown Boveri
ACDA. *See* Arms Control and
Disarmament Agency
ACEP. *See* Advisory Committee on
Export Policy
Administrative exception notes
(AENs), 125
Advisory Committee on Export
Policy (ACEP), 12
Advisory note (AN), 125
AENs. *See* Administrative exception
notes
Aerospace industry, 118–120
Afghanistan, 19, 62, 65–66
Agency for International
Development (AID), 87, 95
Agricultural exports, 43, 65
AID. *See* Agency for International
Development
Air Force Association, 104
Albania, 55
Alcatel telecommunications, 68
American Jewish Congress, 69
AN. *See* Advisory note
Anglo-French List, 48
Angola, 62
Arab countries, 13, 16
Argentina, 19, 25
Armenia/Armenians, 66, 69
Arms Control and Disarmament
Agency (ACDA), 24, 27, 38, 114,
139
Arms Export Control Act of 1976,
22, 117, 147
Arms industry, 8. *See also* Industry
Arms reductions, 82

Asea Brown Boveri (ABB), 111
Ashley, Thomas L., 14–15
Atomic Energy Acts of 1946/1954,
24
Atomic Energy List, 124
Atwood, Donald J., 105
Australia, 52(n7), 109, 141, 149
Australia Group, 141–142, 149
Austria, 81

Bailey Controls of Louisiana, 67
Baker, James A., III, 3–4, 61, 73, 74,
87, 123
Baltic republics, 7, 58, 73
Battle, Laurie C., 50. *See also* Battle
Act
Battle Act, 50–52
Belgium, 46, 132
Berlin, 13, 45
Bilateral investment treaty (BIT), 71,
95–96
Biological weapons, 137, 148
BIT. *See* Bilateral investment treaty
B'nai B'rith, 69
Boeing 747 aircraft, 119
Brazil, 25
Brezhnev, Leonid, 57, 82
Brezhnev Doctrine, 82
Budget deficit, 36
Bulgaria, 14, 44, 55, 58, 60, 75, 83
Bureau of Economic Security, 148
Bureau of Export Administration
(BXA), 20, 21, 32, 38, 147
Bush, George, 1, 2, 63, 65, 69, 71,
74, 76, 82, 86, 97–98, 116, 140.
See also Bush Administration